A PICTORIAL HISTORY OF VAUDEVILLE

Books by Bernard Sobel

Broadway Heartbreak (memoirs)

Burleycue

The Indiscreet Girl (a novel)

The Theatre Handbook

A Pictorial History of Burlesque

A galaxy of vaudeville stars and near-stars as seen by Marius De Zayas. Top row: Eva Tanguay, the "I Don't Care" girl; Sir Harry Lauder, greatest (and thriftiest) of Scottish comedians; Nance O'Neill, a fine tragedienne who often played in vaudeville one-acters. Middle row: Laddie Cliff, a popular English "single" who was known for his distinctive dance routine; Nat Wills, who scratched matches on his beard, and Marshall Wilder, who was facile at telling stories, especially those of other comics; Dainty Marie, who did a striptease on the flying rings; Kathleen Clifford, an early male impersonator. Bottom row: Bert Williams, greatest of all Negro comedians; Charmon, billed as the "Perfect Woman"; Ching Ling Foo, an adroit magician who could bring enough water out of thin air to inundate the stage.

(See over)

For THE LAMBS,

many of whom have helped generously in the preparation of this book

Copyright © 1961 by Lorraine Sobel Lee
All rights reserved
Published by The Citadel Press
222 Park Avenue South, New York 3, N. Y.
Manufactured in the United States of America
Library of Congress Catalog Card No.: 61-18015

Acknowledgments

The following friends helped in the preparation of this book: Arthur Ashley; Herbert Crooker; Donald Duncan of *Dance* Magazine; Ernest Emmerling; Lester Eichel; George Fineberg; Elliott Foreman; Emil Friedlander; Lillian Gale; Paula Gould; Dan Healy; Betty Helm; Fred Hillebrand; Clarence Jacobson; Sam Kaufman; Clark Kinnaird; Gypsy Rose Lee; Leonard Lord; Clarence Nordstrom; Robert Allerton Parker; Jo Ranson; Henry Belmont Rogers; Oscar Serlin; Loring Smith; Jack Waldron; Donald Wayne; Bert Wheeler; Abel Green, editor of *Variety;* George Freedley, curator, and the staff of the Theatre Collection, New York Public Library: Paul Myers, William H. Mathews and Elizabeth P. Barrett; and Howard Lindsay, President of The Players, for the use of the Walter Hampden Memorial Library.

Contents

Index to the Pictures

Many of the photographs in this book are from the author's own collection. Others were kindly supplied by the artists themselves. The Theatre Collection of the New York Public Library generously furnished a great many rare photos. In addition, pictures were obtained from the following sources:

Culver Pictures: Pages 13, top left; 15, right; 33; 35; 83; 89; 95; 96; 98; 132, top and bottom; 136, top; 145; 159; 160; 161; 175; 177; 183; 200, top left; 204, top left; 206, top left and bottom; 207.

New York Daily News: Pages 12, top left; 42; 52; 53; 59; 70; 71; 72; 73; 92; 97, bottom; 99; 100; 117; 123, top; 125, bottom; 130, bottom; 131, top; 134, bottom; 140, bottom left; 155, top right; 157, top; 164; 165, top; 174, left; 180, top left; 184, top; 189, top; 192, bottom right; 193; 201, left; 202, top and bottom right; 211, bottom left; 212, bottom left.

FOREWORD BY *George Jessel*

People like myself—and there aren't many left—who have been before the public for a half-century, are all inclined to favor the yesterdays, and unless they are doing exceedingly well, they live in a capsule of the past, seeing beauty only in that which cannot return, believing to the full that everything that's old is sacred.

However, while I do agree that, in general, show business was much happier then than it is now, because there used to be so much more of it, there are some things that are new that are very good. But it takes an open mind and years of experience to see things clearly, and make them appear in the written word.

This Bernard Sobel is capable of, for he lived most of his life in what Sam Bernard used to call high-class stage business—the years of Ziegfeld—and also in that same era, high-class vaudeville-actors and actresses who, for twenty to thirty years, did the exact same act, and their yearly appearance in each town was looked forward to by the audiences who knew every line of their act, and would sense immediately the addition of a new line or something impromptu. . . . The Avon Comedy Four played a sketch called "The New Teacher" (four middle-aged men with beards in a schoolroom), and to my knowledge, which is pretty near perfect in these things, though lacking in most everything else, they did this act from about 1908 to about 1935! Mr. and Mrs. Jimmie Barry in "The Rube," Cressy and Dayne in "Town Hall Tonight," Barry and Wolferd, Pat Rooney and Marion Brent, McIntyre and Heath, and hundreds of others toured the circuits and in those days, there must have been, in big time and small time, at least a thousand vaudeville engagements throughout the country.

Some of the real vaudevillians have survived the passing of this lost art. . . . Ed Wynn, Eddie Cantor, Jack Benny, George Burns and Gracie Allen, Bobby Clark, Sophie Tucker, Milton Berle, J. Tannen, Bob Hope, J. C. Flippen and myself, and the few others who have been able to transform themselves from old-fashioned vaudeville comics to screen and TV character actors.

Of the newcomers, or at least those who have come up in the last ten to twelve years, only a few, in my opinion, could have stood up with the heroic theatrical figures of forty years ago. These would be Frank Sinatra, Danny Kaye, Jerry Lewis and Dean Martin, Danny Thomas, and in the the lighter vein, Art Linkletter, Jan Murray, George DeWitt and Jack Paar.

However, having lived in vaudeville so many years of my career, it may be I miss seeing some of the forest because of the trees—and as I write this short foreword, I find my eyes filling up with moist memories (this happens to all middle-aged people, whether vaudeville actors or plumbers) and so, with a bit of verse in the manner of Edgar Lee Masters, I'll turn you over to Mr. Sobel. . . . :

Where are Sam Bernard, Eddie Foy, Hitchcock and Weber and Fields
Cliff Gordon, Joe and Ben Welch, the Four Cohans, Al Jolson and all of the
        greats of the two-a-day . . . ?
All are sleeping—sleeping on a cloud over Hammerstein's Victoria
        at 42nd Street and Broadway . . .
Sweetly dreaming and shaking hands with audiences who are so close to them. . . .
Happy that they lived great careers without the aid of microphonic tricks. . . .
Proud that they carried goldheaded canes, proud of Percy Williams, Proctor and
        Keith
—angry with Sullivan and Considine, too;
—puzzled with Pantages, also with Loew. . . .
There they sleep, waiting for a clarion call to awaken them for a brief moment,
        when the statue of George M. Cohan will be unveiled in old new Times
        Square!

PART ONE
The Vaudeville Story

Joe Jackson

Doyle & Dixon

Frank Keenan

Will Rogers

JOE LAURIE, JR.'s ALL-TIME GREATS

George Burns & Gracie Allen   Roger Imhoff & Marcel Corinne

 # Backdrop

Vaudeville is as old as humanity and, in one form or another, will endure as long as people seek laughter, good tunes, mystification and surprise. It is a boost to the spirit, a temporary escape from fear, anxiety and pain. With the decline of the "two-a-day," America lost a rich mine of humor. The troubadours of the vaudeville circuits were the minnesingers of an era; variety's brassy good spirits were a weekly tonic for millions of American—all for the price of a balcony seat.

Why are the memories of a few great performers still so fresh in the national consciousness? Why are certain vaudeville acts recalled long years after they have closed their trunks forever? What made those acts click? Was it skill, showmanship, personality, or material? How explain the inimitable way a certain performer put over a number, the "heart" a singer put into a song, the grandeur an actor lent to an ordinary romantic sketch?

Bert Williams

Smith & Dale

Was it the way a sad clown or a saucy soubrette tugged at your heartstrings or was it a daring acrobatic stunt fraught with terror that you love most to recall? What was it that enshrined the memory of the good old days in your heart—laughter or tears, suspense or artistry?

Ah, days gone beyond recall, with their easy familiarity, the veteran and the newcomer on each week's bill, the stale and the fresh, the ingenuity, satiety, wonder and mystery, the occasional thrill, the happy security of a world within a world—the vaudeville theatre.

Even veteran vaudevillians differ widely in drawing up any slate of the all-time greats. Joe Laurie, Jr., once ventured to draw up an ideal bill (in the *New York Times Magazine*). Just for the flavor of it, here is his glimpse of days beyond recall. "Of course," he admitted, "it is inviting assault and battery to draw up a list because you have to slight a dozen magnificant acts for one you mention, but the bill should be one in which the acts don't conflict, the pace builds up to a smash and everybody has a wonderful time." His nominations included Joe Jackson, the clown cyclist, Doyle and Dixon, dance stylists, "the classiest around for

Willie West & McGinty

Nora Bayes & Jack Norworth

dress, originality and precision," Frank Keenan in a dramatic sketch, 'The Southerner,' Will Rogers, George Burns and Gracie Allen, Roger Imhoff and Corinne, Bert Williams in 'Melody,' Smith and Dale, Willie West and McGinty, Nora Bayes and Jack Norworth in a rendition of 'Harvest Moon.'

Of course, to adopt *one* bill as representative of vaudeville's finest would mean leaving out a host of favorites, but you'll find in this pictorial survey a cornucopia of alternates of all kinds—the long, the short and the tall, soubrettes and sad-eyed "tramp" comics, so you can draw up your own slate from memory and the old programs you've saved from "the good old days." This informal look at vaudeville's varicolored decades cannot hope to provide an encyclopedia or gallery of portraits of all the stars of yesteryear. The old-timers themselves would be hard put to draw up a complete listing of the top billers, not to mention those who never made the Palace but who delighted thousands, nevertheless, along the Sawdust Trail.

Well, how did the pageant begin, and how did its glory fade?

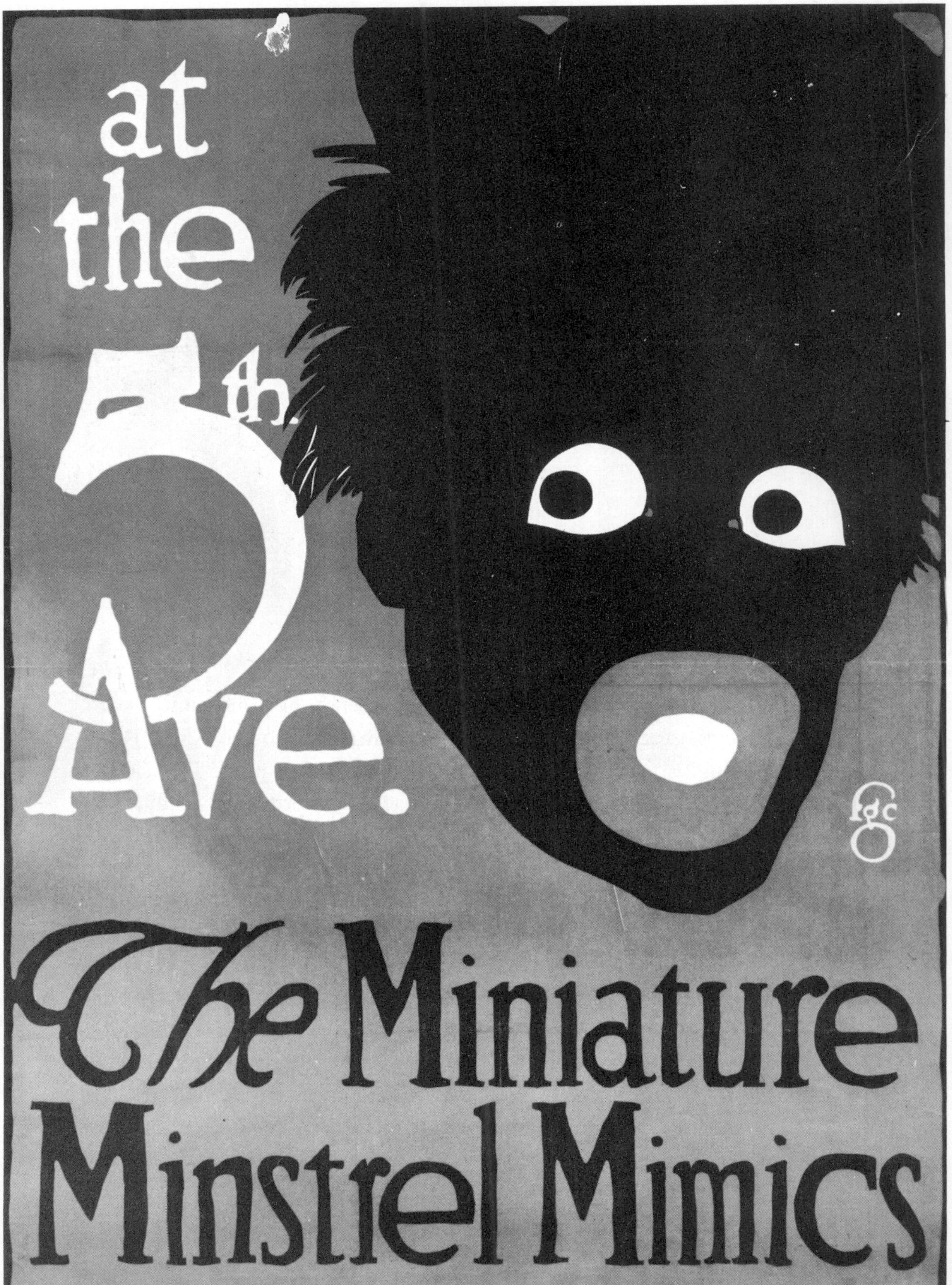
at
the
5th.
Ave.
The Miniature
Minstrel Mimics

Origins and Early Years

It would be fair to say that vaudeville started with the first "single," or solo performer, who successfully entertained an audience, either for pay or just because he enjoyed making people laugh or cry. He might have been a dancer or musician taking part in a Greek or Egyptian rite, a court juggler, an acrobat or magician in the train of a troubadour, or a street-corner mimic.

The term vaudeville itself may have originated with the satiric couplets on the English invaders composed by a Norman workman of the valley of the Vire. Olivier Basselin's *chansons du Vau* or *du Val de Vire* became well-known drinking songs. Still another origin might be in the phrase *voix de ville,* or songs of the city streets.

The word has also been linked to a literary group, the Compagnons Gallois, who composed satirical ballads occasionally dangerously political in theme.

A theatrical company headed by Rozieres which left the Comédie Italienne and opened a Théatre du Vaudeville in Paris in 1792 was frequently in trouble for its topical allusions and had to fall back on semi-historical pieces.

Vaudeville acts also developed from *intermezzi,* short comic dialogues adapted to local taste and performed between the acts of a serious

Popular in the early history of entertainment were the jugglers who performed regularly before crowned heads and were the progenitors of artists like W. C. Fields.

opera. The farces and satirical songs were known as *pièces en vaudeville* and *comédies avec vaudeville* became the staple fare of the French opéra-comique. When these popular entertainments, corresponding to English ballad operas, gave way by the mid-nineteenth century to the vogue for light opera, the word vaudeville came to mean particularly the variety stage on the Continent and the music hall in England.

A Eugène Scribe concoction entitled *Une Nuite de la Garde Na-*

Earliest of the "single" acts was the troubadour, who entertained at court.

tionale was presented as a "vaudeville" in Paris in 1815, and in 1839 a one-act comedy entitled *The Vaudevilliste* was presented at the Théatre de la Renaissance.

At any rate, from its earliest days vaudeville's history is not one of orderly development, era by era, as of growth reflected in stellar personalities. Because of the continuity, versatility and longevity of many of the great performers, past and present may often seem contemporaneous. Some of the luminaries of pre-World War I days are still dominant figures in show business. Young buskers who once sang

A Cheyenne, Wyoming, honky-tonk in 1877.

and passed the hat in honky-tonks or saloons, worked in dime museums, or traveled in circuses and showboat companies have their names blazing over Broadway today.

The incipient American variety show, inspired probably by visiting English performers, took root early here and acquired a certain flair and polish during the mid-nineteenth century about the same time that the distinctively American burlesque or "leg show" was developing from the Black Crook extravaganzas. The assorted acts, or specialties, remained basically the same in character but increased in number and quality by borrowing liberally from the varied forms of native American

"Foxy" Della was the nickname which engaging English comedienne Della Fox gained while playing the United States.

variety entertainment, as exemplified in minstrel or medicine show, circus concert, dime museum, town hall entertainment, beer hall or honkytonk, even, in later years, from the legitimate stage, concert hall, grand opera, ballet, musical comedy and pantomime.

Broadly speaking, there were at first only two kinds of variety shows, those for men only and those for mixed audiences. The "cleaner" shows were held in dime museums, town halls, circus and Chautauqua tents, amusement parks and on river showboats. The more risqué shows were on view in beer-halls, honky-tonks, music halls, burlesque houses and some variety theaters. Both forms contributed to what was to become standard vaudeville.

Of course the variety shows of America had many antecedents in the world of entertainment, both in the old world and the new. Some of these were stationary shows, such as the museums and cabarets, and others were mobile, such as the circuses and wagon shows.

In England vaudeville had flourished during the eighteenth century in what grew to be called music halls, tavern annexes which offered varied programs made up of comic songs, acrobatic acts, conjuring, juggling and dancing. About 1840 an impresario named Charles Morton gave this casual entertainment a more dignified status by presenting it on a stage in a building separate from the tavern itself. Although this type of show was known thenceforth as "variety," it was still built largely around the old-time singing acts. Many an English music-hall star of the nineteenth century was later to add to a homegrown reputation and bank account by transporting the same act for a profitable season or two to America.

In America a circus known as Rickett's opened in Philadelphia as early as 1792. By 1824, John Robinson, whose traveling circus gave performances only during the summer, was concerned enough about his performers to hunt up winter employment for them in all places of entertainment which employed variety players. He was the first theatri-

Fabulous Jenny Lind, "the Swedish nightingale," toured the United States under the management of P. T. Barnum.

cal manager to farm out his performers either as singles or as "packages."

With the expansion of the circus frame from one to two or three rings, the "circus concert" developed. This was a brief entertainment held at the conclusion of the regular performance (for an additional admission fee) in a screened-off section of the Big Top. The programs were usually made up of standard variety acts and included a popular feature—"living statuary." Men and women, coated with a white fluid and wearing white wigs, posed on a revolving platform before a black curtain. Some of these found their way into effective tableaux intensified by gaslight in dime museums and cabaret shows during the winter seasons.

In nineteenth-century America the foreign word "vaudeville" was linked to several playhouses and troupes, but the standard term for entertainment similar to that offered in the English music halls and taverns was "variety." As early as 1769, a group of Philadelphia comedians toured the East in what must have been an early form of vaudeville show. The first "vaudeville house" was opened in New York in the late 1840's by one William Valentine. Astute showmen soon organized traveling variety shows which presented programs made up of singing, dancing and comedy sketches, whetting a continuing national appetite for vaudeville specialties.

In 1871, H. J. Sargent presented a troupe of entertainers known as Sargent's Great Vaudeville Company in Louisville, Kentucky. John W. Ransome used the word vaudeville to describe his touring specialty company in the late 1880's, and it had been the name of a theatre in San Antonio, Texas.

Although the early variety houses encouraged eating and drinking during a show, as the century wore on there was increasing emphasis on the stage show itself, and "top entertainment" began to be advertised. At the turn of the century, variety acts, generally known as vaudeville, were given a variety of appelations—"continuous," "advanced," "electric," "polite," "refined," "fashionable," and "legitimate," to mention a few—many of them stemming from a concerted effort to make it a family entertainment.

The venerable dime museums, which developed from P. T. Barnum's famed institution on Ann Street in New York and which still survive in the byways of Coney Island and other amusement parks, flourished in the 1880's and 1890's. A circuit of Eden and Crystal

B. F. Keith, vaudeville magnate whose name was synonymous with entertainment.

Musées and Wonderlands in cities from coast to coast provided almost continual employment to many branches of the amusement profession. Popular "store shows" in Boston were those sponsored by impresario B. F. Keith and his first partner William Austin. An idea of the kind of entertainment offered in these shows may be derived from the names of some of Keith's original attractions: "Baby Alice, the Midget Wonder" (she weighed one and a half pounds), the "Tattooed Man," the

"Dog-Faced Boy," and the "Three-Headed Songstress" (an optical illusion). In Chicago, Kohl and Castle offered similar entertainment.

One floor of such establishments usually contained a curio hall, where several freaks and platform acts were on view. On another floor was a small theatre, where half-hour to 50-minute variety shows were presented hourly ("Doors open 10:00 A.M.") The usual "orchestra" was a lone pianist. Larger houses offered stock companies in plays, but the smaller ones contented themselves with singers, dancers, minstrels and comics, followed by the barker's cry of "This way out!" to make room for a new audience.

If such a "blow-off" failed to unseat the patrons, a "chaser" (repeating the same act two or three times almost in succession) was often resorted to.

While curio hall attractions, ranging from seven-foot Chinese to twenty-inch midgets such as Queen Mab, Baron Littlefinger, Count Rosebud and Admiral Dot, bearded ladies, spotted or leopard people, bear-, snake-, or gorilla-women, and three-legged boys, and platform acts such as sword-swallowers, magicians, strong-men, and acrobats drew salaries of from $25 to $200 a week, the variety acts commanded salaries of from $25 to $35 for singles and $50 to $70 for doubles. Among such acts were such performers as J. W. Kelly (the rolling-mill man), Hughes and Rastus, and Charley Diamond, a versatile veteran of the Harrigan and Hart shows.

Every self-respecting dime museum had a lecturer, exuding bombast, self-confidence and authority, usually styled "The Professor," who with a grand manner and an ornate vocabulary manipulated a long pointer, schoolmaster-style, to emphasize his discourses on the various "one-of-a-kind acts" and unique freaks seated along the walls of the curio hall—an armless wonder, bearded lady or an Irish sow with fourteen piglets born on the high seas. It was his job to manufacture the high-flown commentary and convince his hearers that what he told them was nothing less than the gospel truth, a feat worthy of his plat-form jugglers.

The goggle-eyed paying customers strolled about, casting a furtive glance at the dog-faced boy, with his blotched white and black skin, or standing enthralled before the intrepid sword-swallower as he satisfied his peculiar appetite for sharp knives and jagged blades, or regarding, with mute horror, the baby embryos pickled in bottles. From the freaks they would proceed to the waxworks, an edifying collection of uncanny life-sized figures of wife-killers, suicides, martyred presidents, poisoners and child wonders, all neatly clad, with waxy, too-pink skins and luxuri-ous false hair, staring sightlessly out at the world.

A maze of mirrors, leading nowhere in an endless yet tempting expanse of quicksilvered cubicles, offered another diversion. At first everyone was confident that he would find his way out, but confusion was compounded by the many false exits. They were not left to ponder too long, however, for the sounds of the orchestra warming up was a sign that the show was about to start.

The typical program began with jugglers, magicians or acrobats, followed by instrumentalists and monologists. The principals in a ro-mantic sketch might reappear, after a speedy costume change, in a song-and-dance specialty. The highlight of the show was often a soft-shoe number preceded by a small boy in uniform who would, with a pontifical gesture, toss a cornucopia of sand before the footlights, to prepare the floor for a gala team of dancers in linen suits, straw boaters and glisten-ing canes.

Even without a roof over his head, a dyed-in-the-wool showman would perform any place, no matter how disreputable, where he could assemble an audience. In the 1870's some performers worked for noth-ing on likely street corners, highways, and vacant lots, on the chance of making a payback on the sale of patent medicines and various elixirs. Many medicine men and quack doctors traveled about the country in

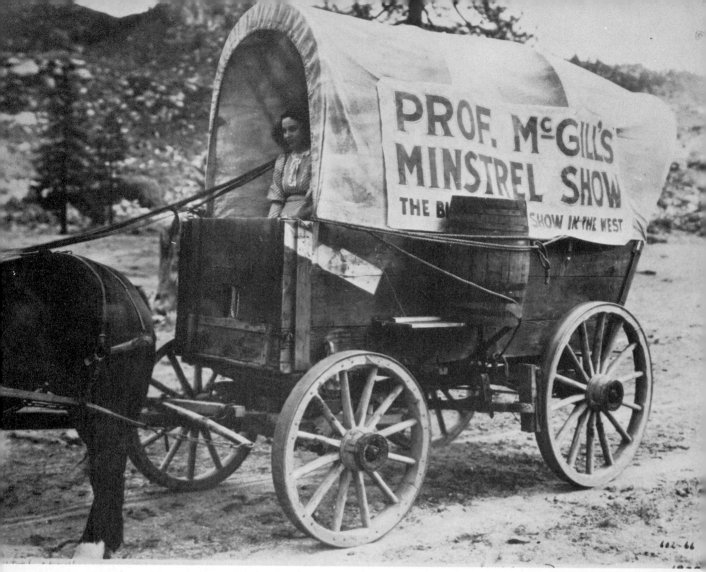

Wagon shows were traveling minstrel entertainment which included variety acts.

wagons, hawking marvelous panaceas with the aid of an entertainer, who sometimes doubled as driver, juggler, singer, or live "cigar store Indian."

Although some states passed laws forbidding such mountebanks to operate, many persistent quacks managed to carry on. By the 1890's some 150 medicine shows were spread across the country. (Even as late as 1911, the Kickapoo Indian Medicine Company brought in a bid of $250,000 when its assets were sold at public auction.)

The humor and the routine of the medicine show varied with the medicine man and his ability to handle the multiple role of master of ceremonies, raconteur and foil. The main feature was usually the musical program—if his cohort could sing a song, strum a guitar, play the mouth-harp, or plunk a banjo. Though the medicine was rarely good for what ailed you, its high alcoholic content plus the free entertainment usually made the purchaser forget, at least temporarily, his indispositions.

A corollary of the medicine or wagon show was the minstrel show, with a cast made up largely of variety performers. From about 1840 to 1880 the minstrel show was the most popular form of entertainment in

"The Come Backs" with George Gale (second from left) and May Hoey. They were the first minstrel show to play vaudeville. The act played Washington, D.C., the night President Garfield was assassinated.

[29]

One-time minstrel man Lew Dockstader was a great blackface single-man entertainer. He was responsible for the popularity of the song shocker, "The Whole Dam Family."

the United States. The plaintive "coon" songs, the sentimental ballads, the soft-shoe dances, the elementary jokes and good-natured repartee were comfortably familiar, like the traditional burnt-cork make-up, striped trousers, straw hats, and banjos.

Along the Ohio River about 1830, Thomas "Daddy" Rice, the father of minstrelsy, introduced his show of popular plantation songs and dances, his face blackened with burnt cork. In his famous "Jump, Jim Crow" number he created what was to become the prototype of the shuffling, improvident Negro—a stock comic figure for the next century.

Incomparable was the comedy which McIntyre and Heath (here the bride and groom) presented as a team or with supporting performers.

Prominent troupes were the Kentucky Minstrels, the Congo Melodists, the Original Christy Minstrels, for whom Stephen Foster wrote songs, the Virginia Minstrels, with whom Dan Emmett introduced the all-time favorite "Dixie," Haverly's Mastodons, Al. G. Field's Minstrels, Dan Bryant's and Hy Henry's. Until after the Civil War these shows did not include Negro performers. Names of performers associated with minstrel shows during their early careers include Lew Dockstader, Primrose and West, Primrose and Walker, McIntyre and Heath, Chaun-

The burnt-cork minstrel, George "Honey Boy" Evans, did a corking headline monologue.

cey Olcott, Eddie Leonard, Paul Dresser (composer of "On the Banks of the Wabash Far Away"), and George "Honey Boy" Evans.

The arrival of a minstrel show was something of a local event, for it usually featured a street parade and sidewalk concert. The minstrels, adventurous, carefree fellows, would jump off the train, dapper in high hats and dusters, kings of all they surveyed. Yet sometimes, when business was bad, their exit from town was not as gay as their entrance. To avoid paying hotel bills some jumped out windows, carpetbag in hand, unless the landlord had had the foresight to outfit his windows with stout iron bars.

From mute variety juggler, W. C. Fields grew into an articulate star of the Ziegfeld Follies and one of the greatest box office draws in motion picture history.

Every minstrel company boasted a female impersonator, who was usually the star, costumed for at least one act in a dress and wig (anticipating Karyl Norman, the Creole Fashion Plate). Many of the standard features of a minstrel show were retained or later revived in vaudeville. The interlocutor, usually in white-face, engaged in banter with the two wisecracking endmen, Mr. Bones and Mr. Tambo. The first part of the show was usually made up of songs, wry conundrums, quips and choruses climaxed by a grand walk-around. The second part, called the "olio," or mixture, was usually a variety bill made up of vocal and instrumental music, dances, specialties, a hoedown and stump speeches.

Master of Irish ballads was the personable tenor, Chauncey Olcott.

Karyl Norman had a record for long runs with his female impersonation entitled "The Creole Fashion Plate."

In the grand finale the entire company participated in farcical afterpieces.

Floating theaters, known as showboats, announced their arrival by a calliope toot on many midwestern rivers as far back as the early nineteenth century and offered popular entertainment to the towns and hamlets where they docked for the night. Many an early actor-manager and his family lived and trouped aboard a flatboat, its roof topped by a flagpole bearing the word "Theatre," the dark interior, lighted by guttering candles, containing a shallow stage at one end and benches

A tense moment during a show boat presentation. (This scene is from the 1927 production of *Show Boat* but captures admirably the flavor of the days of floating theatre.)

running the width of the boat. The standard showboat repertory offered somewhat gory fare, made up largely of rip-roaring melodramas leavened by lighter variety specialties. Similar shows, some shorn of melodrama, continued to be offered as shipboard entertainment for passengers on excursion boats and cruise ships.

The many hinterland town halls which served as community meeting-places for educational, church and political activities also exerted an influence on the development of a trouping tradition by developing and sustaining variety artists. Traveling repertory companies engaged

"The first lady of the theatre," Minnie Maddern Fiske, started her brilliant career as a child performer on a showboat.

to play in town halls interspersed their standard melodrama fare with specialties—magic, singing, dancing and juggling. Many repertory troupes, resident and touring, were known popularly as "ten-twenty-thirties." Their repertoire, like that of the showboat companies, leaned heavily on thrillers, stories of opium dens and white slavery, with the between-the-acts vaudeville easing the tension.

Whitewashed entertainment was often insisted upon by city fathers in cities or churches where theatrical regulations were particularly rigid.

Vaudeville as presented on showboats and in minstrel shows served as morale entertainment on battleships too.

Sunday concert or blue laws allowed singing or reciting but no sketches, dancing, acrobatics or vaudeville which "reflected upon the sanctity of the day of rest." The "sacred concert" tradition was strongly entrenched in Brooklyn and Boston; comic make-up was forbidden, animal acts and acrobats were barred, scenery could not be moved or set up—and tights were out!

For entertainment and a breath of fresh air, patrons might take a ride out of town to a seaside café or an amusement park. Interurban

"Buffalo Bill," Wm. F. Cody, deserted his wild west show to headline for $3,000 a week.

trolley lines linked such restaurants and fairgrounds to nearby towns and their revues and side-shows served as training schools for many future headliners. Some parks featured everything from vaudeville to ballet, with grand opera stars singing arias or singing waiters balancing plates and ballads over the squeaking and grinding of the rollercoasters and mechanical rides and the barkers' gravel-voiced spiels. Many Coney Island establishments and suburban parks offered their patrons vaudeville shows, which meant "skip-and-jump" bookings for vaudevillians also employed by circuses, Wild West shows, fairs and hippodrome spectacles.

But for those who sought the bawdier shows, the side-street honky-tonks, predecessors of burlesque, offered a variety of rowdy fare from the Barbary Coast saloons of San Francisco to the Bowery bars. The smaller places often depended upon eager youngsters, "buskers" who sang songs, clog-danced and passed the hat, to provide free entertainment for the customers. In the higher-class honky-tonks a patron could eat and drink as much as he pleased, indulge in games of chance or sit back and enjoy the show on the stage while a fancy lady flattered him by sitting on his lap—although some such interludes occasionally ended in a brawl when he discovered he was being fondled by a paid female impersonator!

The chorus girls and paid entertainers might fraternize with the customers, but usually the girls of the house were expected to speed the sale of liquor at the tables and to "work the boxes," small private booths draped with curtains that could be drawn. Often a hotel adjoined the honky-tonk, with bedrooms ready for immediate occupancy without benefit of registration. The girls were usually expert in coaxing patrons to order more drinks while they toyed with colored water or strong tea instead of gin or whiskey. At one Silver Palace in Texas the girls would skillfully empty their beer into a trough that flowed back to the bar, where it was rebottled and resold to the same patrons watching the show!

The shows were interminable, often running to twelve or fifteen acts, with the second half of the show continuing until daylight. The opening chorus gave the patrons a tantalizing glimpse of the assembled lovelies, followed by variety acts, singers, dancers, jugglers and acrobats and concluding with an often bawdy afterpiece in which the entire company took part, such as the one which featured a haystack from which a disheveled young couple emerged covered with straw. These skits were usually more risqué than the familiar sentimental skits entitled "After the Shower," "The Villain Still Pursued Her," "The Art of Flirtation" or "My Old Kentucky Home."

A few of the music halls and wine rooms offered well-known entertainers including several foreign stars and better dining service than the honky-tonks. In one establishment known for its choice wines, patrons often asked for the "cork-room," decorated with cast-off corks from bottles of champagne, presenting their theater-ticket stubs for admission.

The evolution from bawdy shows to cleaner ones was not, of course, instantaneous. It was gradual with "big time" vaudeville, featuring important headliners in "class entertainment" and "small time" vaudeville, with performers of lesser stature on the minor circuits. Although some of the small-time circuits continued to rely on slapstick, hokum and "blue" humor, substantially the quality of programs improved, performers' salaries were higher and new theatres replaced ramshackle old structures throughout the country.

A particular offshoot of variety, yet contributory to its development, were the popular Harrigan & Hart shows, made up largely of musical satires and burlesques of current events, but including also vaudeville acts. Tony Pastor made several attempts to compete with them, then realizing he could not do so, concentrated on variety, introducing the first family vaudeville show, one which ladies and children could attend without embarrassment. The success of Tony Pastor's Opera House, on The Bowery, proved that variety could be respectable. Rival managers elsewhere, following his example, hurriedly cleaned up their own bills.

To provide a mounting for the flow of performers, a high degree of versatility in the orchestra pit and backstage was also essential. Orchestra players or a lone pianist had to provide the proper musical cues for scenes of joy, distress or catastrophe, sometimes improvising extra bars to fit a particular act, mood or emergency. Property men were often part scenic artists and part mad geniuses with glue pot, burlap and gilt paint. A stage manager might, if needed, be enlisted as an interlocutor or as a fill-in as a character in a dramatic sketch.

Though they were not vaudevillians themselves, Harrigan and Hart employed variety artists, and contributed directly and indirectly to the growth of vaudeville.

From today's vantage point, the early days of vaudeville in America were crudely unsophisticated; jokes and songs had to be sledge-hammered home. But as Douglas Gilbert summed it up, in his *American Vaudeville*, the fright wigs and red noses, the careening cyclists and banjo-strummers were to bow as show business bloomed and blazoned its way from one red-plush provincial "palace" to *the* Palace in an atmosphere of more subtle sophistication and wit, a potpourri of sparkling personalities, accomplished dancers and vocalists, mimics and monologists, character actors of superb technique.

Gradually the trite, shallow sketches were superseded by more

The father of Ethel, John and Lionel, Maurice Barrymore gave distinction to vaudeville by appearing in one-act plays.

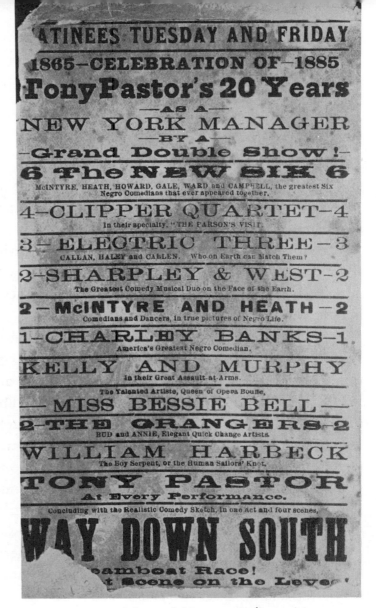

Tony Pastor celebrated his twentieth anniversary as a manager in 1885 with a "Grand Double Show."

literate one-act plays. New dance crazes were reflected in popular dancing and musical numbers, from Salomé to the shimmy. Imported continental stars brought with them an inimitable aura of style and distinction to the bills they graced. Impressed by their success, many leading stars of the American legitimate stage decided to have a fling at vaudeville and engaged prominent dramatists to write special vehicles for their special talents. Even the Barrymores were lured, while top performers received top salaries and billing, at the other end of the scale the popular institution, or ordeal, known as "amateur night" gave many un-knowns their first chance to appear in public. Audiences were unpre-dictable on such occasions; cheers and applause or jeers and a barrage of vegetables might greet the theatrical aspirant, perhaps a cash award and a contract, or "the hook," a long crooked pole which, manipulated backstage, could cut short an act and yank an unsuccessful amateur off into the wings—and oblivion.

Because of its kaleidoscopic quality, it is difficult to encompass, even briefly, the panorama that was vaudeville in its 50-odd peak years from Tony Pastor's salutary experiment to the waning glory of the Palace. The old trunks and albums and yellowed billboards and posters of a bygone era must be sifted sparingly, for who can hope to toast each luminary in that span? Perhaps in lieu of delving into the decades and scattering dusty spangles far and wide, a look at one of Pastor's pro-grams and also at the honor-roll of Palace performers will impart a sample flavor of the pre-neon nineties and the dizzy days just before the talkies "hooked" vaudeville into the wings forever.

The ghostly silence of a once-lively scene underlines the nostalgic images, since we know, as Joe Laurie remarked, that the old two-a-day will never return. "Real two-a-day vaudeville was a *personalized* busi-ness. The actors' personalities reached over the footlights; you could see every change of expression, you could hear every word, catch every in-tonation. No microphones got in the way."

In Pastor's day there were no auditory aids for the patrons in the last row, but the singers could be counted on to belt out their songs fortissimo—with perhaps some help from the audience in a familiar chorus. The average bill usually boasted some 35 performers—songs, dances, acrobatics, mimicry, dramatic and burlesque sketches in rapid succession.

The novel entertainment calculated to attract respectable women patrons and their escorts to Tony Pastor's 14th Street theater was to enrich his many successors. His opening program for the evening of

Tony Pastor, the man who cleaned up variety and transformed it into an entertainment for ladies, gentlemen and children.

October 24, 1881, had eight contrasting acts, headed by Ella Wesner, who sang English music hall numbers with monologue interpolations. Also on his "clean" variety program were the Leland Sisters in a duet; a singer of musical absurdities, Dan Collier; an Irish comic act consisting of songs, dances and "bumps," or hard falls in which Mack sank a hatchet into Ferguson's skull, protected by a trick wig; Lillie Western's performances on concertina, banjo and xylophone successively and an acrobatic-pantomime act in which Frank McNisk performed splits, rollovers and vaults with a chair, a table and a broom. And to see that

"The Bowery Brunhilde," Maggie Cline, Tony Pastor's prize, singing her lusty favorite, "Throw 'im Down McCloskey."

everything went off smoothly—no obscenity or horseplay allowed—there was overseer Tony himself, in high-heeled boots and an old-fashioned opera hat which opened with a snap, ready to sing a selection from his repertoire of some 1,500 songs. He knew the value of sentiment and familiarity. Many other performers learned that the public—of

Hay Ward who did a tramp act called "Harold and Percy" with Harry
Vokes at Tony Pastor's in 1887.

those good old days—expected acts polished to a shiny-pants gleam—
but the same pants, hat and cane, or whatever the familiar hallmark
might be. Many established acts continued practically unchanged for
years, sharpened to perfection. Moore & Littlefield presented a skit entitled "Change Your Act or Go Back to the Woods" for a quarter-century.

But there was a restlessness by the time vaudeville reached the
years of its greatest magnitude. The time was ripe for bolder innovators
attuned to a lively ragtime tempo and the ripostes and wisecracks of a
man-about-town rather than a "Dutch uncle" comic.

J.S. BERRY'S BROADWAY THEATRE

DRAMA VARIETY

Broadway and Fourth Street, Williamsburgh.

F. A. McCLANE .... MANAGER | ALF A. WALLACE .... Director of Amusements

CARD TO THE PUBLIC.--Monday, May, 30, Grand Inaugural of my Summer Season. Hoping, by strict attention to business, and presenting only such talent as I know to be worthy of your patronage, to merit a continuation of your favor, I remain the Public's Obedient Servant, F. A. McCLANE.

Monday Evg., May 30, '81

Every Evening at 8. Matinees Tuesday and Saturday at 2.

THE TALENTED YOUNG AMERICAN ACTOR, MR.

ALF. A. WALLACE

In his great Sensational Drama, in Three Acts, entitled THE

HIGHWAYMEN OF PARIS

CARTOUCHE, the Highwayman	ALF A. WALLACE	Lion	Ed. Kane
Gribishon	F. A. McClane	Casson de Late	A. Harte
Count D'Arbarne	David Roach	Mr. Bodilet	Dave Callahan
Marquis DeGrandlieu	Gus H. Saville	Louise	Mable Cole
Red Judas	George Harris	Can Can	Grace Bunnell
Francis Carroll	John H. Byrne	Eugenie	Ethel Mead
Le Loup	Tom Granger	Madam Babilet	Annie Cummings
Ferret	T. Boyd	Soldiers and Peasants by the Company	

ACT 1—The Post Neuf. River Seen and view of Paris by right. The Ambrosio's. Francois is protected by Cartouche. A 000 francs reward for Cartouche. Interview between Cartouche and his betrothed. The trial in Judas. Expulsion of Judas from the gang. Hotel of the Marquis D'Grandlieu. The Marquis and his young portrait. Meeting between Eugenie and Francois. Visit of Capt. at the to the Marquis. The robbery. Unexpected appearance of Count D'Arbarne. Race of Cartouche. The tables turned. Lodging of one can. Ferret. vacates vranel and her mystery lover. A singular visit to a secret warning. Discovery of the gentleman robber. Escape of Cartouche. Humble lodging of Louise. Francois informs his views of his stolen debts. Timely interference. The pursuit. Cartouche affects his escape by the ordinary. House tops and bird's eye view of Paris. Cartouche stands at bay. Taken in his toils. One more defies his capture. "The prison is not built that can hold Cartouche the jay boy." ACT 2—Prison Cell and Pavean or Cortelon. Cartouche in prison. His picture and bravado. The jailor Judas and his treachery. Cartouche stricks a bargin with Judas. Gribishon visits the prison in disguise. Plot to recue Cartouche from the cells. Thirteen escape of Cart nullifying torture. ACT 3—Country near Paris. Cartouche at large. His remarkable encounter with M. Judas. The final. Farm House and Corn Fields. Preparation for the marriage of Cartouche and Louise. Gribishon follows his captain's example. Visitors to the farm. Recognition of the stolen jewels. Cartouche in the toils once more. His escape. Ferret in Paris. The traitor on the watch. The fatal shot. Death of Louise. The pursuit. Catacombs of Paris. Cartouche gallantly defends his Gang. The attack. Death of the Robber Cartouche—and impressive Tablea.

RETURN OF THE VETERAN TO THE SCENES OF FORMER TRIUMPHS

ARCHEY HUGHES

THIS GENTLEMEN STANDS PRE-EMINENT AT THE HEAD OF ALL OTHERS AS THE DELINEATOR OF THE OLDEN TIME NEGRO

FIRST APPEARANCE OF THE PRINCE OF SONG AND DANCE ARTISTS

TOMMY GRANGER

IN HIS NEW AND ORIGINAL SPECIALTY, PAROLE'S RIDER, BEING A LIFE LIKE IMITATION OF A JOCKEY AFTER A RIDE ALSO HIS GREAT REEL FOR AN EIGHT DAY STOVE

THE METROPOLITAN FAVORITE, THE CHARMING SONG AND DANCE LADY

ANNIE CUMMINGS

FIRST APPEARANCE OF THE PREMIERS OF MUSICAL COMEDY

GUS H. SAVILLE

LATE BRYANT & SAVILLE AND THE FAMOUS COMEDIAN, WIT AND PUNSTER

JOHN H. BYRNE

Late Shirley & Byrne, in their great original comedy creation, **The College of Music**, introducing all the popular airs of the period on the Xylophone, Airophone and the Diplomated Organ and Saville's Electric B flat Cornet Solos, in which he stands pre-eminent above all rivals, and Byrne's mischievous and incomparable rendition of the Mocking Bird upon an ordinary Tin Whistle.

FIRST APPEARANCE OF THE CHARMING AND ACCOMPLISHED ACTRESS

ETHEL MEAD

OUR GREAT STOCK COMPANY.

F. A. McClane, George Harris, Dave Callahan, David Roach, Mable Cole, Ethel Mead

The Advertising of this Theatre is done by the Washington Advertising Company of 36 Morton Street, Williamsburgh.

EXTRA NOTICE.—Every FRIDAY will hereafter be known as

AMATEURS' NIGHT!

When in conjunction with our regular Company, Amateurs may appear in what specialty they chose and the best Amateurs in their respective lines will receive a handsome present. During the evening the following laughable games will be introduced **Apple Ducking, Pie Eating and the Great Candle and Apple Trick**

LADIES' NIGHTS

Hereafter, every Tuesday and Friday Night, Ladies, when accompanied by Gentlemen, will be ADMITTED FREE.

ADMISSION, ... 10, 15, 25 CENTS. | BOXES .... 50 CENTS

Cameron & Co., Steam Theatrical Printers, 9 Ann Street, New York.

3

A Vaudevillian's
Life and Times

During its Golden Age, vaudeville represented a facet of middle-class American life, along with fraternal lodges, baseball games, socials and picnics. In 1910 there were some 2,000 small-time hinterland theaters. There was Shakespeare and there were literature clubs and sedate theater parties—and there was vaudeville.

From Jersey City to Kalamazoo, vaudeville symbolized unpretentious enjoyment, abandonment to the folksy humor of slapstick, pratfalls, comic make-up, pride in the recognition of wheezy jokes, the satisfaction of beating the comedian to the tag-line and joining in familiar choruses. It was a comfortable belt-loosening familiarity.

Of course, the fans had their favorites. They could rattle off catchlines and bits of stage business, and many could almost repeat entire acts themselves. The typical audience was an easy-going one— alert, earthy, responsive and friendly. Having a good time was every man's right, like the divine right of kings. And the vaudeville patron was king of all he surveyed, a two-bit critic, but certain of his own judgments, ready to applaud or ignore. He was a member of one big happy family, ready to marvel or to guffaw.

Except for an audience which sat on its hands, vaudevillians disliked only one kind, the rowdy collegians who would go on a rampage after a football game, damaging theater property and breaking up a performance, in some cases even harassing the performers themselves. Some theater managers subdued rioters by turning sprinklers or firehoses on them. The manager of one theater electrified the railing surrounding the orchestra pit to prevent overexuberant patrons from jumping onto the stage. In one college town, students entered a vaudeville theater carrying alarm clocks set to go off simultaneously, calculated to turn the regular performance into a temporary bedlam.

The usually genial audience out front, holding its sides with laughter, gave hardly a thought to the combination of hardships and hopes

GRAND OPERA HOUSE

ELM PLACE near FULTON ST.

Week Commencing Monday, Dec. 23
1896

| WEDNESDAY— | MATINEES | —SATURDAY. |

Direct from the Chicago Auditorium,

THE TROCADERO VAUDEVILLES

10—EUROPEAN NOVELTIES—10

Headed by
the Peerless **SANDOW** His Farewell!

Presenting a refined vaudeville and athletic entertainment, patronized by the best class of theatre-goers in America and recognized by press and public as a performance without a peer in number, quality and variety of acts, and special individual features.

Congress of World-Famous Artists and Athletes.
Greatest Physical Lesson of the Age.
Conceived, Organized and Promoted by

F. ZIEGFELD, JR.

PROGRAMME

Descriptive Piece—"A Hunting Scene."....................P. Bucalosi
   Description—The morning breaks. Calm and Peaceful. The Huntsman prepares for the pleasure of the Chase. Our Huntsman sounds a merry blast. Echo. The Parties join. A Hunting we will go. Barking of dogs. Tally-Ho. Full Cry. The Death. We return home. A Hunting we will go.
March—"The Real Thing"....................................H. W. Petrie

HERR AUGUST DEWELL
The Eminent Scandinavian Gymnast.

THE LUCIFERS
Grotesque from the Alhambra, London. Mr. Lucifer, champion combined high kicker and jumper of the world. Mr. Lucifer's muscular development has been attained in one year under Sandow's System of Physical Culture,

STACK and LATELL
Premier Triple Bar Performers. First Appearance.

N. E. KAUFMANN
The champion bicycle trick rider of the world and holder of every existing championship and who has appeared before most of the crowned heads of Europe. Mr. Kaufmann is ready to defend his title at any time against all comers for any amount at two to one. He originated all his novel feats and odd wheels.

MONS O'GUST
The Eminent French Clown, from the Follies Bergere, Paris, presenting his marvelous imitations. His first appearance in America. Mons. O Gust enjoys the distinction of being only French artist who has ever appeared before the Emperor of Germany. Many have tried to equal his Trombone Solo-Imitation, but pale into insignificance beside this great artist

5—THE FIVE JORDANS—5
Misses Mamie, Rosey. Nelly, Messrs. Lewis and August. Performing the most graceful and daring aerial acts ever witnessed.
   Mr. Ziegfeld requests the indulgence of the audience for the short delay necessary in placing the net, which entirely precludes the possibility of any accident befalling the performers.

INTERMISSION FIVE MINUTES.

THE GREAT AMANN
Europe's greatest impersonator, introducing life-like reproductions of world-famous men, including America's greatest statesmen. The management desires to call attention to the remarkable work of this truly great artist. Having devoted a life-time to the study of character impersonations, he is able to produce life-like representations of the world's most famous men. The inspired look of the poet, the thoughtful mien of the statesman and the determined countenance of the vicious warrior, are given with such stating fidelity that it is difficult to realize it is all the face of one man. Special attention is called to Amann's impersonation of Svengali, without the aid of any artifice except wig and beard Mr. Amann makes up for this character in less than half a minute, the the time required by Wilton Lackaye being two hours, and his portrayal of this character has astonished all artists.

BILLY VAN
Comedian.

Curtain will drop one minute to allow for setting the stage for Sandow.

Performance concluding with
!! SANDOW !!
THE MONARCH OF MUSCLE.

Mr. Ziegfeld offers $10,000 to any athlete duplicating Sandow's Performance, Mr. Sandow will select his programme from the following superhuman feats:

Physically perfect. Acknowledged by anatomists to be the strongest man in the world. History does not record among the great gladiators of ancient Rome a man with such muscular development as Sandow.

His 400 wonderfully developed muscles are exhibited in the following manner:
   Muscular repose (all the muscles relaxed.)
   Muscular tension (all muscles firm as steel.)
   Abdominal muscles when tense, producing the wonderful checker-board arrangement of fibers, existence of which modern anatomists deny, being plainly visible at a distance of 300 feet.
   The Biceps (muscles of the upper arm), the Triceps (muscles of the back of arm) the Deltoid (muscles of the shoulders), the Trapezino (muscles which raise the shoulders).
   The muscles of the back showing plainly all three layers.
   The action and uses of the different muscles.
   The chest expansion; Sandow's chest measurement is 47 inches, expanded it is 61 inches, an expansion of 14 inches. The greatest expansion known at the Olympian Games in Rome was 6 inches.
   Sandow will exhibit his extraordinary command over his entire muscular system by making his muscles dance.

   NEW.   NEW.   NEW.

   The world's greatest acrobats have found it almost impossible to turn somersaults landing on the same spot they spring from, and only a few have accomplished it, and to perform this feat with weights has never been a tempted. Mr. Sandow stands alone in accomplishing this feat with 56 pounds in each hand.
   The audience will hardly realize what the announcement that Mr. Sandow will turn a complete somersault from the knees means, and it is only his enormous and unequalled strength that enables him to perform this feat with 56 pounds in each hand.
Lifting with one Finger 750 Pounds Dead Weight from the Ground.
   The Muscle Dance still further demonstrates the absolute control Mr. Sandow has of his muscular system, and the enormous strength in his individual muscles. He will compel his Biceps to dance with 90 pounds attached to each Bicep.
   Resisting the dropping of 90 pounds attached to chain from each thumb, arms extended, weight doubling at the drop of each foot.
Holding Out at Arm's Length, Mounted Byclist in each Hand.
   Resting only on neck and heels and holding four men on body. Those who do not appreciate how difficult this feat is, can easily convince themselves by attempting it without any weight resting on the body.
   Mr. Sandow's performance concluding with his new feat entitled,

TOMB OF HERCULES.

SANDOW bearing upon his body a weight of 3200 pounds, composed of all the paraphernalia used in his performance with his attendants added.

   "To Mr. Henry E. Abbey, of New York, and Mr. F. Ziegfeld, jr., of Chicago, great credit is due for providing the American public with such entertaining and valuable stimulant to encourage physical development as Sandow's performance produces."—Inter-Ocean, Chicago, October 6th.

EXECUTIVE STAFF FOR MR. F. ZIEGFELD, Jr.

E. D. Stults..Representative
G. Salde ina..Musical Director
August Fewell..Stage Director
Ed. Maxwell..Stage Manager
Frank Wickward..Master of Properties
Harry Jordan..Machinist
Martin Hayack.....................Master of Properties for Sandow

Sandow, The Strong Man, upholds his title on a typical vaudeville bill which includes Billy B. Van, musical comedy star; The Great Amann, protean artist; Mon. O'Gust, French clown, making his American debut; and The Five Jordans, whose aerial act required a short delay so that the placing of a large net would preclude any accident befalling that graceful, daring performance.

Vivid characterizations, ranging from school teachers to lusty old men, were "Chic" Sale's forte. His nationally popular outhouse humor book was a best seller.

that made it possible for the hard-working performers behind the foot-lights to give them an evening of varied entertainment. Depending on their degree of applause, acts were tried and shaped to some degree in the network of hinterland vaudeville houses. But many a performer was in himself a complete microcosm of show business—actor, producer, writer and director, all rolled into one. "A man was his own creative force in the old days," reminisced Fred Allen, "and his own boss." He

The acidulous humor which Fred Allen dispensed was softened by the charm of his wife, lovely Portland Hoffa. His autobiography, *Much Ado About Me,* is a theatrical masterpiece.

was boss at least of his own act, which if he were a true showman he would polish to a diamond-sharp perfection.

Without being lawless or disrespectful of the law, the true vaudevillian was really a law unto himself. Any hostelry where he hung his hat was home. He might bicker over billing or dressing-room priority, but on the road he was always ready for a laugh or a practical joke. Show people added a dash of spice to the towns they visited. Their colorful presence at railway depots, bars, restaurants, boarding-houses and hotels quickened the sleepy small-town pace. Their trunks might be shabby, but their clothes were flashy and their womenfolk were painted, powdered and bejeweled—even if the jewels were paste. Those vaude-villians fortunate enough to have a thick skin were unmindful of stares and sly looks. The hope of better prospects ahead helped them carry on when despair might have thrown them. Instead of getting jittery, the "never-say-die" trouper would lean on his self-conceit, his violin case or his trained dog and face circumstances with a shrug or a swagger.

These gay visitors who called perhaps once or twice a season in the smaller cities were a "down-to-earth clannish group, with fewer swell heads than the ordinary run of actors," as Gene Fowler remarked. Edward Fenton, in his *Vaudeville Theatre*, called them "a faithful, hard-working lot, living in the land of fancy, inclined to be egotistical, yet sensitive; temperamental, yet with here and there a disconcerting strain of foresight; often envious or jealous of the progress or success of fellow artists; easily influenced and quick to take offense at real or fancied be-littlement of their particular act or style; ambitious for success"—but, alas, frequently taken advantage of on occasion by an unscrupulous manager or agent because of a lack of shrewd judgment in business deal-ings, such as signing a contract.

The lives of touring variety actors were far from easy. They often were obliged to travel at odd hours to meet split-week engagements. They might have to appear in several theaters a night, with only the sketchiest of rehearsals. At each new theater, whether it was a one-night stand or a week, they had to adapt themselves anew to the peculiarity of the conductor, the orchestra, the stagehands and the all-powerful manager. They had to put up with all sorts of dressing-rooms and hotels, with unheated wings and indifferent lunch-counter cooks, with cindery train-trips and jolting street-car rides, with winter snowdrifts and de-layed baggage and dog-days and melting make-up.

They had to share, at close quarters, the society of performers who were appearing on the same circuit, an association that sometimes led to quarrels and clashes over billings. Temperamental binges were common in the theater, where some ruthless tactics often proved necessary to gain and maintain supremacy. There were also sporadic incidents where a lazy or thoughtless performer could snarl a rehearsal by showing up late, drunk or sans music and costume. But after the backstage fireworks peace would reign again for a while and those at odds would dramatically "kiss and make up"—until the next row. Such a fracas was usually caused by personal antipathy, seldom by discrimination because of race, color or sect. Ability was the password for inclusion in footlight fellowship, and camaraderie the keynote on the occasion of an opening night for a fellow performer. But the well-wishing telegrams avoided the phrase "good luck," which in show business, like whistling in a dressing-room, putting a hat on a bed or sighting a bird on a window sill, is regarded as unlucky.

Pinning down a vaudeville booking could be a heartbreaking procedure, with actor, agent, booker and manager all hanging on the lifeline of the performer's acceptance by a fickle public. The test of any act's position on a bill came after the first performance, for in spite of contractual arrangements, if the act didn't go over, the manager put it in the spot he thought suitable. Or threw it out.

Most managers weren't particularly concerned with what happened to an actor. The box office receipts were their prime consideration and their attitude toward an actor depended on how useful they considered him to be to the current program. But to the actor, a week or split-week run represented his stage life. If he made good, he had a good chance of carrying on. If he failed, his career might wither on the vine.

The agent, who represented the actor, made the contact with the booker, or sometimes directly with the theater manager. Small-time agents in the employ of a big-time agent, might fork over a percentage

A group of vaudeville artists, composers, writers and comedians at a gathering in 1927. *Seated left to right:* Jack White, Lou Schwartz, Heywood Broun, Arthur Brown, Frances Williams, Lou Davis, Jr., J. Fred Coots, Harry Rosenthal, Willie and Eugene Howard. *Standing:* Tom Patricola. *Seated front:* Rose Perfect, Harry Richman.

of his bookings and also have access to the big-time agent's lists of acts and could submit them to smaller circuits if they had any open dates. The agent's job was no cinch. When he helped make a performer a star he might be praised extravagantly; if not he was continually "on the rack," blamed and repudiated. But agents often discovered, nurtured and even supported promising performers until they reached a point at which their talents were salable. Among the experts in this intricate game were Jim Hodgson, Max Hart and Arthur Klein, the latter of whom became a successful producer of revues.

In the early days, saloon-keepers, bartenders and restaurateurs often acted unofficially as talent scouts to insure that their patrons were well entertained while dining or drinking. But theatrical agents made the selection of talent a full-time business, following performers from one theater to another in order to gauge their proteges' effect on different audiences, giving them advice on gestures, telling them how to dress and how to talk to managers. Agents sold their services as negotiators, fought for the best terms and top billing. The Rialto dubbed them "ten-percenters," and such a fee for the services of an agent or booking agency became standard.

In the parlance of show business, all the cross-country sawdust trails led to the booking office which supplied acts for the Palace in New York, where the Albee office had developed a system for weeding out acts who braved the famous Monday matinee. Those who failed to make good at the first performance were dropped with a "no interest" rating. "Pick up" meant a chance at a trial run and the magic words "the route" meant a solid booking over the entire Albee circuit.

"The Death Trail" and "The Aching Heart" were the names by which performers sardonically referred to those small-time circuits notorious for their heartless managers, uninspired beaneries and miserable hotel accommodations. Sometimes a manager would engage more acts than were needed, give the actors a try-out, cagily determine which ones were best suited to the local community and fire the others without paying them a cent. One theater manager would walk over to the stove and shake it loudly when he heard an act he didn't like, a signal to the stage manager that the actors onstage at the time were fired. Another manager interrupted a two-man team before they had rehearsed their first musical number. "You're through," he said, although they protested that they had been engaged for the week. "I happened to be on the train you came

A scene from a typical tabloid musical as produced by Anatole Friedland. The "tabs," which started around 1911 and flourished through the 1920's, were short musical comedies that played the vaudeville circuits.

in on," was the reply, "and I heard you rehearsing your songs. That was enough for me."

The road to financial success was seldom a straight one, and only a few performers amassed sizable "takes." Salaries on the big-time circuits were determined principally by bookers who decided where an act should be placed on a bill. Usually acts were permanently categorized and "an opening act was an opening act from the day you were an amateur until you quit the business to open a delicatessen." An opening

King of minstrel men was Eddie Leonard, who could never leave the stage until he sang "Roley, Boley Eyes."

act usually could count on an engagement at from $150 to $200 a week. This was usually a team of acrobats, balancers, tumblers, jugglers or knockabout comedians or an animal act. Such silent acts seemed best suited to the inevitable "warming-up" period that audiences seemed to require. The number two act, usually a singing-and-dancing act with some patter performed by a couple drew a salary of from $225 to $250. The next-to-closing act, if not a star, but still *the* attraction on the bill, would get $350 to $500, while a star could command $750 to $1,500. This might be a flash act, a comedy act, with a single comedian or a straight man and a comic. If an act was fourth or fifth on a big-time bill,

Children's acts were popular in vaudeville. Here are two child stars who went on to higher fame. *(Left)* Louise Hovick, who later became the incomparable Gypsy Rose Lee; *(Center)* Lillian Roth (with doll) and her sister

it was a sure next-to-closing act on the small-time circuit. In small-time vaudeville salaries were of course less: the number one act would get about $150 top, the number two $175, the number three $300 and the next to closing $350, the closing $200 to $450 if a "flash." Bookers regarded performers as headliners, sure-fire next-to-closers, standard acts, playable and fill-ins, when there was nothing better available.

Naturally there was a need to leave a vivid impression on the audience and many performers adopted devious techniques to prolong their few minutes in the limelight. Although the spotlight was originally saved by the performer for the climactic moment in his act, many performers acquired such an inflated opinion of their own importance that they demanded the spotlight be focused on them throughout their act. The same goading vanity affected bows and curtain calls. A performer might

Anna; *(Right)* Joe E. Brown *(far left),* who made his stage debut as one of the Five Marvelous Ashtons.

leave the stage reluctantly, leaving one hand or foot in sight at the edge of the proscenium arch, or change hats or coats for new ones until his wardrobe was exhausted. Eddie Leonard played perpetual encores on an ominous farewell note. "This may be my last time around. You never know," he would say, or he would ask the audience, "Do you want to hear 'Roly Boly Eyes'?" then, instead of responding to this request, would sing "Little Brown Baby" or another popular song, holding out long beyond the time due him. The business of taking innumerable bows and making curtain speeches was finally curtailed, at least at the Palace, by signs posted backstage reading, "You must take only two bows."

But vaudevillians, bless them, were irresponsible, and the more "don't" signs, the more ways they figured out to outwit attempts to keep them within the rule book.

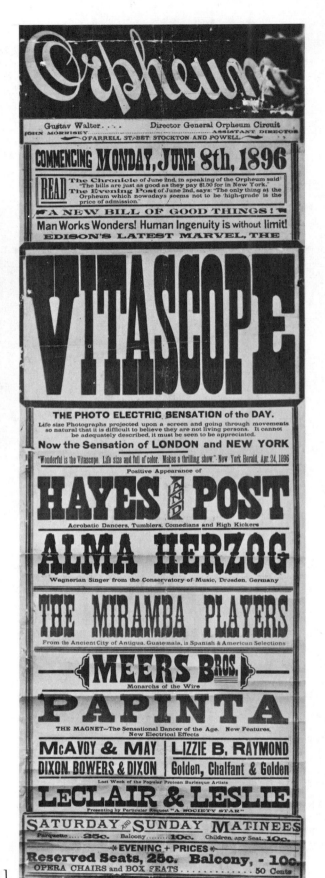

An 1896 poster for an Orpheum circuit theatre—one of Martin Beck's far-flung chain—announces a showing of a new invention that would contribute to vaudeville's decline—Edison's wonderful Vitascope.

Czars of the Circuits

The major vaudeville circuits were manipulated by a few all-powerful moguls, while the affiliated minor circuits cooperated through the central metropolitan booking offices and also through a protective association of vaudeville managers. A few theatres were operated locally, in the same manner that independent small-town merchants today operate outside the great store chains.

Several of the important magnates who controlled the prime showcases for vaudevillians' talents started their careers on the stage or in the circus ring. Tony Pastor, who sought and got first-class patronage both for his road shows and his "clean-as-a-hound's-tooth" 14th Street Theatre show, was a show business veteran with a bottomless repertoire of good will and songs. He had once been a singing clown with a circus. Martin Beck came to the United States from Germany as master of a theatrical troupe. F.F. Proctor started as an acrobat, B.F. Keith as a barker and grifter, and E.F. Albee left Barnum's to take a small show on the road himself.

Each was remembered for his attitude toward performers and the public—austere or expansive, genial or vindictive. Beck, known for his

Throughout the history of the Palace, E. F. Albee was the dominating force. He was important also as a builder of great theatres.

bite, nevertheless raised the standard of vaudeville by his readiness to pay big salaries to concert musicians and ballet dancers, declaring that a lot of people *liked* good music. Hammerstein's prices fluctuated, depending on how much he thought the traffic would bear, some sensational novelty and freak attractions drawing more of the curious than others.

But until they decided to sell out and retire from active participation in show business—spotting, selecting, channeling and promoting their hand-picked hopefuls and headliners—such activity proved an all-absorbing interest throughout their long and frequently lively careers. One top-hatted impresario might pursue temperamental actresses across an ocean and back, while another, once dubbed the "king of small time," might specialize in ornate fittings for the ladies' rooms in his theatres, but their common concern was box office receipts in the black.

Early vaudeville magnate and theatre builder was F. F. Proctor.

Several of these show-business czars were at one time or another rivals and partners, depending upon the amicable financial settlement of franchise claims or competitive bookings.

The history of the robber barons who dominated the metropolitan houses and major circuits may be described as a crazy-quilt, with patches of skulduggery, fraud, good faith, and betrayal. Although the principals have long since passed from the scene, they still exercise a fascination in an age dominated by corporations rather than individuals. The highlights in a chronicle of this internecine warfare may perhaps be reduced to an account of the feuds and battle tactics and at least a mention of those whose operations were conducted with less rancor and less publicity.

The tycoons raged, connived, outwitted and cursed each other but suffered comparatively minor personal inconvenience. Most of them sold out and retired wealthy to nurse their bruised pride or angry spleen.

But their titanic struggles for power involved everyone from the haughtiest headliner to the humblest member on the bill. And in the end the throttling of competitive circuits by consolidation helped to bring about the demise of old-time vaudeville.

Dominating the scene for many years was E.F. Albee, whose reign as czar outlasted many rivals. His goading ambition and ruthless methods were to cost him many friends and associates. His most profitable partnership was with B.F. Keith, although as he grew in power he made many other liaisons, such as the one with Western producer John J. Murdock, which were useful in gaining his objective of supremacy.

His association with Keith began with two Boston theatres and culminated in 1925 with the ownership of a circuit involving some 350 theatres and 20,000 performers. By the time of Keith's death in 1914, Albee had already taken over full control. As a result, the name of Keith, even though it was displayed over the illustrious Palace Theatre, had dwindled in importance, while the name of Albee had become synonymous with vaudeville.

Teaming up together in Boston about 1885 in a museum show, they replaced the freaks with a phenomenally successful Dutch low comedy team (Weber and Fields) and put on a repertory of Gilbert and Sullivan musicals publicized by Albee with the query, "Why pay $1.50 when you can see our show for 25¢?" There was surely a future in vaudeville if it could be promoted as a form of family entertainment . . . so their program formulated itself.

Albee built his first important theater in Boston in 1893, with money borrowed from the Catholic diocese on the promise of "'clean" shows. On the opening night, patrons were invited to tour the handsome structure from the auditorium to the cellar, which boasted a whitewashed coal bin! This venture was so successful that Albee, in conjunction with various partners, began to open more theaters, the finest vaudeville structures in the world—the Albee in Brooklyn, the Palace in Cleveland, the Memorial in Boston—all famous for their marble lobbies, green rooms, oil paintings and new system of ventilation.

Albee's progress to virtual dictatorship was characterized by the shedding of old associates and by a deliberate effort to impress the theatrical world with his importance as general manager of the Keith circuit and as head of the United Booking Office. By 1923 he governed the entertainment of approximately 4,000,000 people by his far-flung grip on houses and performers. It is not surprising that thousands hated him for his often-expressed contempt for actors. He relished his power to hire and fire. "All my life actors have been gypping me," he announced at the time the U.B.O. was founded, "and now I'm going to gyp them."

"The Ol' Massa would really put it on for you," Groucho Marx wrote recently. "When you were eventually ushered into his august presence, the stage would be all set. In his private lair the carpet was thick and silent. His desk was about eighty feet long, or so it seemed, and on it there would be nothing but an expensive vase containing a single rose. The only chair in the room would be the one occupied by the master. The poor actor, trembling with fear, would stand there before him, shuffling his feet like a schoolboy who had just been caught redhanded swiping the teacher's lunch. In this setting the actor would humbly listen while Albee informed him what his salary would be for the coming season."*

Albee made his own rules. If he didn't like the material in an act, it was out, for he had a contract which gave him the authority to censor any word, line, business or costume which violated his idea of decency. (After he gained control of the Palace, he exercised this veto power by cancelling Nazimova in "The Unknown Lady," as well as a play concerning fraudulent divorce laws.)

Albee's whipping boy at the Palace was his chief booker, adroit,

* Groucho Marx, *Groucho and Me*. New York: Bernard Geis Associates, 1959.

E. F. Albee's influential aide was the dextrous booking agent,
E. V. Darling.

diplomatic Eddie Darling. He served as a buffer and a liaison agent,
keeping headliners' tempers soothed and keeping order backstage. In
one backstage clash between two actresses over the No. 1 dressing room,
Darling, unable to placate them, since both demanded the prize area,
solved the controversy by a trick. He placed buckets of paint and step-
ladders before dressing rooms No. 1 and No. 2, pretending that they
were being redecorated. As a result, both stars had to dress elsewhere
and peace was restored.

Albee's path to power was far from a peaceful one—to cite only a few of the skirmishes and campaigns in which he was involved through several decades. Although several vaudeville theaters flourished after the turn of the century in New York, including Hammerstein's Victoria and Proctor's Fifth Avenue Theater, the Albee-Keith empire considered itself virtually a monopoly and acted accordingly. For example, in 1907 the Keith Vaudeville exchange induced a major competitor, Klaw and Erlanger, to keep out of vaudeville for ten years for a generous financial consideration.

This arrangement withstood a suit by a prominent agent, Max Hart, but in 1912 a spectacular feud erupted which involved a president of the United States, Theodore Roosevelt. Sir Harry Lauder had been booked to appear at the Erlanger-controlled Belasco Theatre by William Morris, a longtime foe of Albee and monopoly. When Albee, on the basis of his secret treaty with Klaw and Erlanger, demanded an immediate cancellation of the act or the forfeiture of $25,000, Erlanger reluctantly prepared to comply. After Morris brought the matter to the attention of the President, "trust-buster Teddy," with characteristic energy, called the manager of the Belasco and told him if Lauder were not permitted to play the house he would instruct his Attorney-General to start action against the theatre trust at once. Albee was forced to concede defeat. At one time William Morris induced Klaw and Erlanger to join him against Albee in what was called "legitimate blackmail." Klaw and Erlanger proceeded to buy up Albee's stars. He was forced to buy them back—and did, in a costly triumph.

Another conflict between William Morris and his arch-enemy Albee arose when "Sime" Silverman, the publisher of *Variety* and always a champion of fair play, sponsored Morris's efforts to increase actors' rights. The actors' association known as the White Rats was a particular target of Albee's ire. He tried to put *Variety* out of business by publishing his own paper, the short-lived New York *Star*. He also declared that

For many years, Marcus Klaw was a partner of A. L. Erlanger. They headed the most powerful theatrical syndicate of their era and gave employment to many vaudevillians in musicals and legitimate plays.

any actor caught reading *Variety* would be blacklisted and anyone advertising in it would be barred from the United Booking Office—an edict comparable to issuing a death warrant in show business.

Although he built many magnificent theaters, Albee acquired a black reputation for cutting actors down to size, slicing salaries, restricting freedom of movement, blacklisting on impulse. In order to break the White Rats' strike, which began as more of a fight of actors against

King of producers, A. L. Erlanger brought scores of vaudevillians into musicals during the heyday of The Great White Way. Considering himself a Napoleon, he liked to fraternize with political notables. Here he lectures Governor Miller of New York.

managers but ended as a desperate fight of actors against actors, Albee and other managers spent millions of dollars on a campaign which was "fronted" by a few actors whose cooperation they bought for the price of "a good route and good money." As part of their campaign strategy they organized the National Vaudeville Artists, known as the N.V.A. and also as "Never Vev Albee."

Its overt purpose, as Albee professed, was to build up the theatri-

The inspired publisher of *Variety*, the "Bible of Show Business," Sime Silverman, was the Gibraltar of justice to the actor. The causes he championed and won are representative of the finest aspects of the amusement world. His beloved protegé, Abel Green, carries on the Sime tradition, impartially, accurately and comprehensively—that is, practically over all liberty-loving continents.

cal profession. But in order to insure membership he issued an order that before a performer could get a contract for any theater governed by the N.M.P.A. (the National Managers' Protective Association), he would have to forswear the White Rats group and become a member in good standing in the N.V.A. To make sure that his edict was carried out, the managers rented an apartment directly opposite the White Rats'

Urbane and beloved Charles E. Dillingham employed stars like Will Rogers and Marilyn Miller, vaudeville graduates, in his Broadway musicals. He was one of a managerial triumvirate which included A. L. Erlanger and Florenz Ziegfeld.

clubhouse so they could check up on actors who went in and out and subsequently blacklist them.

As Joe Laurie, Jr. recorded the episode in his *Vaudeville*: "Soon the members got wise to what was being done, and little by little the attendance fell off, the dues stopped coming in and the club had to take a mortgage of $5,000 on its furniture. That soon was spent, and the bank made them a proposition: they had a 'certain party' that would take over the property and even pay the clubhouse debts. The Rats had

Long identified with vaudeville circuits was the powerful personality, J. J. Murdock.

to take it. It turned out later that the "certain party" was Albee, who paid off the bondholders."

Masking his treachery under a cloak of benevolence, Albee arranged through his secretary, Henry Chesterfield, to woo actors with kind deeds. He established a committee for hearing actors' complaints, put on huge benefit shows, directed the ushers in his theaters to make collections for N.V.A. members, handed out $1,000 death benefits and, following a plan originated by William Morris, built in 1930 the N.V.A. tuberculosis lodge at Saranac. But when vaudeville business began to go downhill Albee had no further need for the N.V.A. and when the members, no longer able to maintain the club, moved across the street, his interest turned to hatred, which he nurtured until his death.

Out of the abortive efforts of the valiant White Rats, however, came a resurgence of the battle for actors' rights. After 1934 Equity took up the challenge from them and has since wholeheartedly devoted itself to bettering the welfare of members of the theatrical profession. Today, AGVA guards the fortunes of the vaudevillians.

In contrast to Albee's cavalier attitude toward performers was that of one of his contemporaries, F. F. Proctor, who was one of the first managers to provide decent dressing-rooms, modern heating and ventilating systems. Although he seldom went backstage, he left $1,000,000 to the Actors' Fund at his death in 1928. While he was still active in the theatrical world he joined with Charles Frohman to form the Frohman Stock Company, which featured legitimate stage stars such as Maude Adams, John Drew, Billie Burke and Otis Skinner.

Born in Maine in 1852, Proctor's youthful athletic abilities attracted the attention of a veteran circus acrobat and he soon won swift recognition as an acrobat, balancer and juggler of globes, pyramids and barrels. Success as a performer, however, was not his primary interest; he wanted to build, own and manage theatres. He began to collect capital by obtaining a popcorn, candy and lemonade concession. His ambition grew along with his earnings, which grew so quickly that he was soon running several theaters.

His first New York spot attracted masculine patrons by the easygoing invitation: "At our temple of fun, we do all to please. You can smoke your cigar and drink at your ease." Later he termed his show "polite vaudeville" and offered mixed audiences what he called "star-studded" variety shows at prices of ten, twenty and thirty cents. A catchy slogan advertised both his 23rd Street Theatre and his policy of continuous vaudeville, inaugurated in Boston by B. F. Keith: "After breakfast, go to Proctor's; after Proctor's, go to bed." (Although the

From cloth-sponger to millionaire vaudeville circuit and theatre chain impresario comprises the history of Marcus Loew.

building no longer stands, a sidewalk plaque marks the site of his popular place of entertainment.) He offered an additional inducement to early theatregoers—the early-bird matinee, with all seats in the orchestra and balcony available until eleven o'clock in the morning at reduced prices.

The Shuberts' business competition was never a threat for czar Albee. They put forth one venture in 1909 and another, known as "advanced vaudeville," in 1920. When straight big-time bills failed,

S. Z. Poli and his enterprises governed the policy of the small-time circuit.

Lee Shubert changed his entertainment to "unit" shows, condensed revues and musicals. After a battle with Albee over acts and theaters Shubert finally booked some of his shows into burlesque houses, but by 1923 his "advanced vaudeville" collapsed, leaving scores of bankrupts among the burlesque house managers.

One of the strongest contenders in the West was Martin Beck, who began his career in San Francisco, where he was associated with the Orpheum Theater. He perfected a procedure, eventually adopted by the entire industry, initiated as early as 1880 by Harry Miner and Thomas Canary, that of a linked chain or circuit of consecutive bookings. Complete programs were thus transferred from one city to another. By 1905, Beck's Orpheum circuit included seventeen houses from the Coast to Chicago. He was largely responsible for starting the Western Vaudeville Association and for linking the Orpheum circuit with that of Kohl and Castle, Middle West vaudeville potentates.

One Western circuit changed hands several times, from ownership by Timothy D. Sullivan and John Considine to Marcus Loew and back again. The partners were challenged for a time by Alexander Pantages, who soon owned a theater in every town where the two had formerly held sway. Also active was Sylvester Z. Poli, who started his career as a manufacturer of wax exhibits and a museum-owner, building up a fortune before retiring from show business.

But Albee remained undisputed czar of major vaudeville, though Beck made an effort to challenge his hold on Eastern circuits by buying a chain of six Eastern theaters from Percy Williams, who had made a name for himself as a dime-thriller author (*Tracy the Outlaw,* etc.). Albee nosed Beck out of the deal by buying the chain at a higher price, topping that coup by purchasing a share of the Keith-built Palace from Meyerfield, president of the Orpheum circuit. Holding only a quarter-interest in the Palace, Beck retired from vaudeville to direct and produce plays for Klaw and Erlanger.

But though it seemed Albee was king of all he surveyed, he wasn't able to raise the curtain on his new possession, the Palace, until he came to terms on the matter of a franchise with Oscar Hammerstein I, owner of the Victoria, long one of the outstanding New York vaudeville houses. Here were introduced an array of freak and "nut" acts, featuring a variety of individuals in the news—Arctic explorers, bicycle racing champions, famous fighters, wrestlers. Hammerstein, known for his

Oscar Hammerstein, pioneer vaudeville magnate, who sponsored the Roof and the Victoria.

"plug" opera hat, Van Dyke beard and omnipresent cigar, gave the Metropolitan Opera a run for its money with his rival Manhattan Opera House. The glass-walled Paradise Roof atop the Victoria was the special province of his son Willie. The show, billed as "Hytone Vaudeville," included amateur nights and special nights, with afterpieces by a cast composed of all the performers playing downstairs in the Victoria.

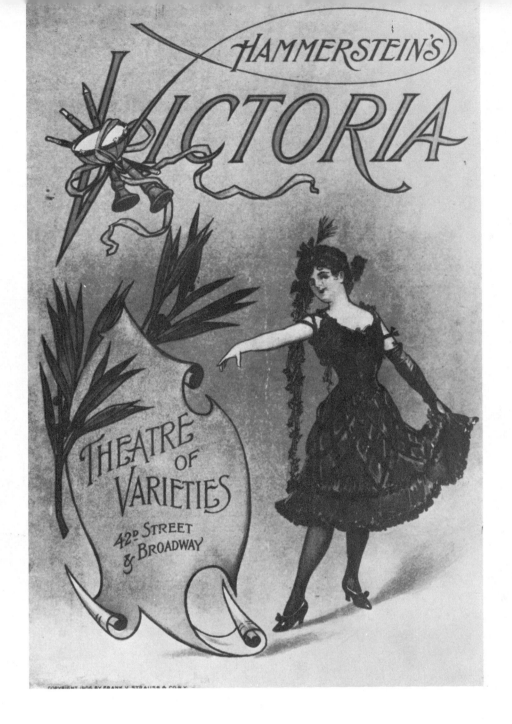

When Albee bought out Hammerstein's franchise—for $200,000 —it was Willie's unchivalrous prediction that the Palace wouldn't last two years. But though an ingenious showman, he was a poor prophet. The Palace stayed open long enough to become the most famous vaudeville house in America, while the Hammersteins' pride, the Victoria, folded in less than a year.

NEXT WEEK, MONDAY, FEB. 10

First Appearance at the Victoria in Three Years

GEORGE EVANS

"THE HONEY BOY"

Dolan and Lenharr

Comedy Skit

BESSIE WYNN

Comedienne

Mlle. Chester And Her Educated Statue Dog

First Time This Season

Ryan & Richfield

"MAG HAGGERTY'S FATHER"

Emma Frances
And Her Whirlwind Arabs

Marno Troupe
European Acrobats

| Slater & Williams | New Vitagraph |
| Colored Singers and Dancers | Views |

First Time at This Theatre

W. C. FIELDS

Unique Comedy Juggler

(Left) The cover of the program from Hammerstein's Victoria and *(right)* a typical bill from that theatre.

B. F. Keith's Palace Theatre, New York

Ed Wynn, "The Perfect Fool," appeared on the first bill at the Palace. He subsequently initiated live radio shows, becoming a national figure as "The Fire Chief." He is one of the most versatile artists of the era.

5

The Palace Era

By the time the Palace offered its first "class" matinee on March 24, 1913, audiences were being handed a little more sophistication than the Pastor potpourri. The first bill at the Palace was as follows:

THE PALACE GIRLS
Dance ensemble

OTA GYGI
Spanish Court Violinist

LA NAPIERKOWSKA
Pantomimist and dancer

SPEAKING TO FATHER
Comedy skit by George Ade, with Milton Pollack

THE ETERNAL WALTZ
Flash act based on operetta, with 30 people including Mabel Berra and Cyril Chadwick

McINTYRE & HARTY
(Retired after Monday matinee and replaced by:)

TAYLOR HOLMES
Monologist

FOUR VANIS
Wire act

HY MAYER
Cartoonist

ED WYNN
Comedian

After weeks of failure, the "Divine Sarah" Bernhardt, one of the greatest actresses of all time, made the Palace bills successful and helped establish American vaudeville.

But the publicized "high class" and the higher prices ($2.00 a seat, a dollar more than the admission price at a rival house, Hammerstein's Victoria) did not begin to pay off for the Palace impresarios until the advent of Sarah Bernhardt, though she was well past her prime, going on seventy. Still, the "divine Sarah" proved alluring and magnetic in her scenes with Lou Tellegen. Thick-piled bear rugs laid from her dressing-room to the stage muffled the sound of her wooden leg. She refused to play on the same bill with animal acts or blackface

PALACE $2 VAUDEVILLE A JOKE: DOUBLE=CROSSING BOOMERANG

$7,000 Variety Program in New York's Most Extravagant Theatre Falls with a Thud. No Praise and no Attendance. Direction of House Thrown on "House Manager" to Evade Liability or Connection for Unscrupulous Move Made by Big Time Managers in Upsetting Their Own "Franchise."

The fate of "$2 Vaudeville" at the new Palace, New York, was sealed before the house opened Monday. Since then its doom has become accepted along Broadway. Monday afternoon, following an expenditure of $4,000 for preliminary advertising of the initial variety program ($1,500 of which was spent in the Sunday papers) the Palace failed to draw capacity, even with the great quantity of "paper" given away. In the evening the Palace held capacity on the orchestra floor but was not filled upstairs. About one-half present received free coupons.

Tuesday afternoon but three rows in the orchestra were occupied. Tuesday night all the people in the house would not have filled the first ten rows downstairs. Wednesday afternoon business had dropped to even less and Wednesday people with passes for the Palace were displaying them as they purchased tickets for the show at Hammerstein's.

The Palace opposes Hammerstein's Victoria at 42d street and 7th avenue, five blocks away from the new theatre at 7th avenue and 47th street. With all the usual "deadheads" overflowing Hammerstein's on a Monday afternoon over at the Palace that day, the sale of standing room had to be stopped Monday afternoon by Willie Hammerstein upon orders from the fireman detailed to the theatre. Monday night Hammerstein's played to capacity and repeated it twice Tuesday, with a program costing nearly $1,000 less than the Palace's, although Hammerstein's bill has seven more acts.

The news of "the Palace's flop" pleased the regulars around New Times Square mightily. Everyone knew of the double-crossing tactics employed in the opening of the Palace. It had commenced its career with a vaudeville show in face of the "franchise" issued by the United Booking Offices to the Hammerstein theatre for the Times Square section of New York City. As all the big time in the United States and Canada is allied with the U. B. O., this franchise was supposed to protect Hammerstein from invasion. All the biggest of the big time managers are connected with the Palace. The Palace "job" will go down in theatrical history as attempting the most brazen and unscrupulous piece of double-crossing ever recorded in theatricals. That it has not and will not succeed doesn't redound to the credit of the violaters of contracts and franchises, but is wholly due to the undeniable fact that the big time managerial heads know how to put over anything in the show business excepting a show.

Whoever arranged the opening program for the Palace presented the poorest big time vaudeville show New York has ever seen. It's also the worst exhibition of showmanship New York has known. Martin Beck assumed the responsibility for it last week, but when hearing the universal expression passed upon the opening program before it was shown, he sidestepped. Wednesday, Beck was crying "this is only the first week," and he ought to have a week longer to follow out his ideas. On top of this colossal failure of the Palace, Beck is expected to sail for Berlin any day now.

Though Beck and Albee disclaim connection with the direction of the Palace, placing the blame upon the house manager, Frank Thompson, who is an intimate friend of Paul Keith, Beck is still looking for acts for the Palace bills, and Albee is also on a search for headline attractions. An effort was made Tuesday to secure Fritzi Scheff and Frank Keenan for next week's Palace bill. Monday Albee was in the theatre attempting to convince those he came in contact with that he had no interest in the theatre, although during the matinee when discovering a door would not properly work in the basement, Mr. Albee raised a fuss about it.

The effort to prevent a direct connection being traced was probably for the purpose of setting this up as a defense if William and Oscar Hammerstein, holders of the U. B. O. "franchise," should bring an action in equity to restrain the Palace from opening. It is said the Hammersteins had no such intention. When Willie Hammerstein saw the announcement for the opening program he is reported to have taken a day off, the first in several years. The vaudeville people claimed Willie booked the Palace show himself, but this Mr. Hammerstein smilingly denied. A betting book was made up last Friday, $100 to $75 was offered the Palace would be the first big time house in New York to close this season, and $100 even the Palace would change policy before reopening. Tuesday even money was offered in any amount that the Palace policy will be altered by April 7. This was based on a story the Palace people were sending for legitimate producers to talk over the future of the house. Another circumstantial story had it that a United official who twice visited the Victoria, came to open indirect negotiations with Willie Hammerstein to take charge of the Palace.

One of the many peculiar features of the current Palace bill is that a $1,500 act (Napierkowska) is featured above the costliest turn on the bill ("The Eternal Waltz") at $3,000. None of the acts listed was known to the New York public and outside of the readers of VARIETY no one here had ever heard of Napierkowska, who came from the Orpheum Circuit.

It is estimated that the Palace, New York, will lose $8,500 on this week's show, without the extra advertising. It costs $5,000 weekly to operate the expensive house. The program costs $7,000. If the Palace has a good Sunday business it may do $3,500 on the week. Prices range from 25 to 50 cents in the gallery to $2 in the boxes. At Hammerstein's the usual prices are one dollar, and at Loew's American (8th avenue and 42d street), the front seats in the orchestra may be secured for 25 cents. Monday Mr. Loew is said to have received a wire from a prominent theatrical man congratulating him on the opening of the Palace, although no one around believes Loew would take the Palace for pop vaudeville.

The cost of operating the $850,000 Palace by the year is $110,000. Against this would be offsets through rental income of about $25,000 leaving the rent for the theatre itself $85,000 per annum. At this price and with only a seating capacity of 1,800, no legitimate manager will entertain the proposition. Another bar to the disposal of the house for production purposes is the size of the working stage, 29x65, about the same as the stage at the Comedy theatre, known as a "parlor house."

The New York dailies did not treat the Palace very kindly. Extracts from the notices on the opening by the critics are appended.

PRESS OPINIONS ON THE PALACE.

The opening bill did not lend much enthusiasm to the occasion. The first part of the entertainment is a long-drawn-out affair of poor vaudeville numbers that drag, and a very bad miniature musical comedy that lacks even the quality of a burlesque. The second part of the show, however, is much better, though many yesterday did not wait for it.—World.

Yesterday the intentions of the management were plainly of the best, but the fulfillment did not make the sort of an entertainment which is going to attract attention to the new theatre.—Sun.

In such an auditorium the opening programme of variety acts presented a rather sorry contrast. Only one number on the long bill even slightly resembled a novelty. This was "The Eternal Waltz," which other cities of the United States have seen this season. Through a long afternoon the first audience waited and waited and waited.—Herald.

Will A. Page is the press representative for the house. He is ~~~~~~~

This story from the "Bible of Show Business," Variety, reflects the inside attitude toward the Palace following the opening.

Lou Tellegen played opposite Sarah Bernhardt in vaudeville; then married and divorced Metropolitan Opera star, Geraldine Farrar.

comedians and demanded $500 in gold at the end of each night's performance. Her $7,000 a week net salary set a high-water mark until 1931, when banjo-eyed Eddie Cantor, who rose rapidly from a last-minute substitution to a top-drawing name, drew $7,500 a week gross for nine weeks on a bill he shared with George ("Hello, Mama") Jessel and Burns and Allen. In 1915 he was only drawing $275 a week as a member of the team of Cantor and Lee.

After its modest start on the outskirts of the theater district, on

Pat Rooney made the audience gasp when he first did the waltz clog. He and his wife, Marion Bent, presented one of first vaudeville musical tabloids, "Rings of Smoke."

the site of a torn-down millinery shop and next door to a saloon, the Palace became the undisputed Tiffany's of show business. A well-loved showplace, it cost more than a million dollars to build and served for some nineteen years as the acme of show business. The office floors above the theatre soon became a hive of booking agents and 47th and Broadway was also referred to as the "Palace Beach," where many an unemployed vaudevillian might be found strolling or window-shopping, whether "at liberty" or just "laying off for a while."

Pat Rooney, Sr., who played the Palace more often than any other

The Four Cohans, Jerry, Helen, Josephine and George M., inseparable for many years.

performer, called it "the home plate of show business." He recalled that all the while performers toured the country playing small houses, then bigger ones, they "always hoped for the day when they'd make the Palace," for it would mean that they had gone all the way around the bases.

For the public it signified the cream of vaudeville, "a weekly certainty of seeing a good show, perhaps even a great one." Because of an expectation of quality, a performer had to prove his act was worth more than peanuts or a perfunctory clap. He had to leave 'em gasping or crying and eager for more.

Despite the aura of a Palace booking, audience pressure on performers at the Palace could be so nerve-wracking that some veteran performers, such as the Four Cohans, declined to play there. Al Jolson, a Shubert exclusive property, never essayed it. Each member of the

The greatest of all "mammy" singers, Al Jolson was also a superb comedian known for multiple encores, always prefaced by his slogan, "You ain't heard nothing yet." He made the first talking musical film, *The Jazz Singer*. He also made millions and bequeathed millions to charity.

audience confidently took it upon himself to pass on the latest offerings, offering his comments to all and sundry during intermission, whether it was an old favorite to be welcomed back, a new crop of jokes to be appraised, a new dance team to be rated. Everyone wanted to be the first to proclaim who stole what line from whom or to pick out the most promising new luminary or soon-to-be waning star.

The regular Monday matinee audience was tough, but ungrudging with applause. About 75% of the yearly business at the Palace came from its subscription list. Reserved parquet seats downstairs were in demand and the illustrious audience usually included agents, critics and Broadway producers, such as Florenz Ziegfeld, Charles Dillingham, David Belasco, Winthrop Ames and the Shuberts. The whole theater was aglow with anticipation and a palpable tension as the overture was concluded and the familiar spell of enchantment settled over the footlights. A back-kick, a high note, a belly laugh, a pratfall or a daring stunt could bring down the house in a sudden, delirious release.

It was here that a vaudeville performer could reach the pinnacle of achievement. Among the familiar acts that most of the fans knew by heart were also a handful of starry-eyed hopefuls braving the heady Palace atmosphere for the first breathless time. The big-time performers who repeated often all had loyal followings, but many beginners had to prove themselves to win that "diploma of merit" that proclaimed prestige. The Palace was almost a royal portrait gallery of eminent vaudevillians. The passing parade brought forth many stars whose names would blaze for years on theater, movie and broadcasting studio marquees after vaudeville's lustre dimmed. Many entertainers of stature got their first real "break" at the Palace. Jack Benny started as the violin half of an act called Benny & Woods in a next-to-opening spot. After seven years in the "bush leagues" in the West, he made the Orpheum big-time and headlined a Palace act in 1929. Dancer Ray Bolger was discovered in a Gus Edwards revue at the Palace and Hildegarde made a mark there as a pianist. Fanny Brice, of Follies and "Baby Snooks" fame, saw her name as one of the first to go up in lights at the Palace over Broadway.

Usually nine varied acts comprised the weekly bill, with an intermission. The performers usually met to renew "auld acquaintance" with colleagues and stagehands and to check music and light cues at a Mon-

Fanny Brice doing her burlesque of the Martha Graham type of modernistic dancing.

Starting as a vaudeville performer, Jack Benny made a brief flight into a Broadway review, then became one of the most popular stars of radio and television. Jack's comic signature is simulated miserliness. His partner in this picture is Janette Hackett.

day morning rehearsal. Rough or slow spots were generally smoothed out before the evening show by the house manager, who kept a firm watch on running time and strove for a well-balanced program. By midweek the acts were in solid shape for the Albee circuit bookers, who gathered to cull the most promising and weed out the also-rans.

For a palmy decade or more patrons settled back comfortably

Creator of the "Schooldays" acts, Gus Edwards was responsible for the discovery of more young talent than anyone ever associated with vaudeville.

against homelike flowered cretonne seats to enjoy on the stage some of the greatest performers of the last half-century. When the crystal chandelier blazed again during intermission they gathered in the marble lobby (to be modernized with zebrawood when movies displaced live performers as the magnet) to compare impressions on the merits of this week's show over last week's. The tradition of top entertainment at the Palace continued unchallenged for as long as vaudeville bills maintained a supremacy. Virtuoso after virtuoso filled the spotlight, concentrating all his or her individual artistry in a brief turn. But the tide of mass entertainment engulfed the perishable talent that sparked so many silent stages into uproarious laughter or unabashed sentiment.

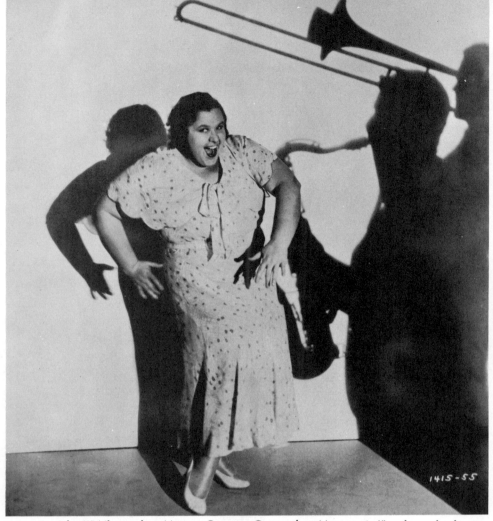

Kate Smith ("When the Moon Comes Over the Mountain") played eleven consecutive weeks at the Palace.

By the time of the unsettled late twenties, audiences had turned from theaters to the more freakish and ribald entertainment available at outdoor piers and pavilions in a blowsy, happy era of flagpole sitting, rocking-chair contests and dance marathons. In 1927 the part-talking movie version of Raphaelson's *The Jazz Singer*, starring Al Jolson, proved the voice of doom.

Variety mused gloomily in its columns on the fall of vaudeville. "When Vaude was king," one story ran, "the bills cost from $10,000 to $12,000, and at a $2.00 top the Palace clocked a regular $500,000 a year profit. But as show costs pyramided profits dwindled and it was inevitable that the Palace would either have to go vaudefilm or straight film."

Working usually single, Lou Holtz augmented his Yiddish monologue, at times, with girl foils.

The last years of fading vaudeville at the Palace were marked by futile efforts to attract patrons by presenting honky-tonk afterpieces in which all the acts took part and by introducing prominent guests from the audience. The once-dignified showplace also featured small-town "Country Store Night" giveaways. In 1928 the management even tried placing an electric piano in the lobby, hopeful that it would lure a few.

Yet in August, 1931, Kate Smith set an all-time two-a-day record, remaining at the Palace for eleven weeks. Lou Holz, Lyda Roberts and William Gaxton managed to stay for eight. But after an all-star bill with Eddie Cantor, Georgie Jessel and Burns and Allen, the last straight vaudeville show at the Palace floundered to a halt on July 9, 1932, with a bill which included, among others, Louis Sobol, Harry Richman and Lillian Roth. A shaky mesalliance of vaudeville and movies extended the dimming lustre of the Palace a few years longer, but the tiny

In 1931 Eddie Cantor and George Jessel teamed up to break all records at the Palace.

Looking every inch a queen, Sophie Tucker, "Last of the Red Hot Mammas," made her early variety performances with band accompaniment.

Record-breaking Palace headliner William Gaxton also starred in *A Connecticut Yankee, The Music Box Revue,* and the Pulitzer Prize-winning musical *Of Thee I Sing.*

One of the greatest mimics in vaudeville history was Elsie Janis. She starred in *The Fair Co-ed* and *The Silver Slipper* with Joseph Cawthorn. Her imitation of Will Rogers in his rope act and her superb dancing the audiences will never forget.

#1 dressing room over which so many temperamental stars had quarreled was more often dark than not.

But the memories of a host of memorable stars, from Nora Bayes, with her dazzling stage presence and unaffected warmth, Sophie Tucker's red-hot mama delivery, appealing Elsie Janis, rope-twirling, good-natured Will Rogers, warbler Eddie Leonard, the nimble-footed Astaires, Gallagher and Shean and Smith and Dale, Doc Rockwell, Frank Fay and Joe Cook, twined like an unwithered laurel around its name, though

Gallagher and Shean, whose song bearing their names brought them enduring fame and Follies stardom.

trunks of props got dustier, stage door johnnies dwindled and backstage lights almost dimmed out forever in the twilight of show business as the old vaudevillians knew it.

With the closing of standard vaudeville after nineteen star-studded years, the Palace began a definite decline that was reflected in the engagement of lesser performers and a combination film-and-vaudeville policy. The last two-a-day vaudeville show accompanying a screen attraction on January 7, 1933, featured Marie Gambarelli, for many years

Trick apparatus and his imaginary four Hawaiians, made Joe Cook an all-time favorite and led to musical comedy stardom.

a prima ballerina of Roxy stage presentations, Bobby Murphy, the bird-imitating Arnaut Brothers and the lightweight champion Benny Leonard.

The Palace held to a straight picture policy from February 11, 1933, until April 2, 1933, when it began playing pictures and vaudeville on a continuous show. The last combination of this type was presented during the week of September 20, 1935. Then, after a four-

High in the ranks of popular mimics was Eddie Garr.

teen-year interval of motion pictures only, vaudeville returned to the
Palace on May 19, 1949, on a combination bill with first-run pictures.

On October 16, 1951, came a bombshell who, like Bernhardt before her, "packed them in." A single star took over a good half of
the bill, supported by, among others, the veteran comedy team of Smith
and Dale. Together, singer Judy Garland, and two-a-day made one of
the most memorable comebacks in Broadway history. Booked for four

The inimitable clown Poodles Hanneford did an uproarious equestrian act.

Continuously fascinating was Will Mahoney's "falling down" number and his dance on a xylophone.

Though one of the most popular Yiddish stars ever to grace the stage, Moliy Picon deserted this domain occasionally to charm variety's audiences.

weeks, she stayed 19, breaking Kate Smith's record of 11 in 1931. For her, too, all the roads in show business led to the Palace's once-hallowed stage. She opened to a thundering ovation and through her tears told a happy audience, "Since I was a kid the one thing I've dreamed of was playing the Palace. It is like finally reaching the promised land."

Some wiseacres predicted that even with Judy Garland's magic that the Palace's revival policy would soon fail. It ran, however, for some seven years, during which time 300 eight-act shows were pre-

Helen
KANE

BERNARD
SCHMITTKE

Helen Kane's squeak and her "boop-a-doop" style precipitated an army of imitators, not one of them as good as the original.

sented, providing a measure of employment for those performers who made up the 2,400-odd acts.

Among those presented during the revival days were Lillian Roth, the "I'll Cry Tomorrow" girl, Phil Spitalny and his orchestra, Gus Van,

Like many other famous artists, Judy Garland started her career as a child performer in vaudeville, one of the Gumm sisters. Later she became a world-famous motion picture star. Then, happily, she returned to vaudeville to initiate the revival at the Palace, where she established again the popularity of the two-a-day.

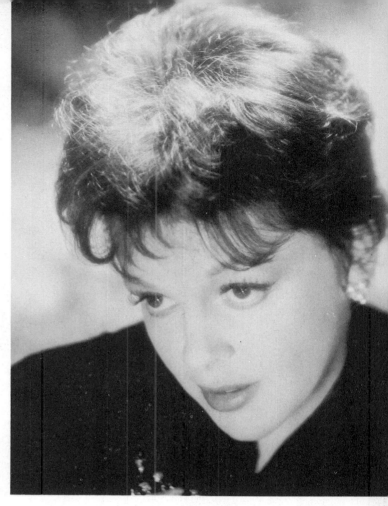

who had been a fixture of the Follies with Joe Schenk, Eddie Garr, a mimic, Hal Sherman, Buster West, the clown Will Mahoney, Poodles Hannaford, Molly Picon, Joey Faye, comedian Lew Parker, Orson Bean and the "Boop-Boop-a-Doop" girl, Helen Kane. A touch of red-carpet glamour was supplied by a bill featuring Metropolitan Opera star Lauritz Melchior in a comedy act, with Helen Traubel soon following suit with gravel-voiced Jimmy Durante.

Perhaps, like a wise old phoenix, the Palace will continue to provide a stimulus and a hospitable atmosphere out of which came countless great vaudeville bills past, out of which a tradition of top entertainment has infused each generation of new entertainers with a respect for the once-brightest bellwether of show business, still doing business at the same old stand. The Palace will be ready for vaudeville's next comeback —but soon there may not be enough solid-hit old-timers left to make up a crackerjack bill. *Sic transit gloria.*

Milton Berle, who began his career as a vaudeville juvenile, reigned as the "Mr. Television" of the medium's early years.

Exit Vaudeville –

Enter Television

Many reasons have been advanced for the collapse of vaudeville, some of them major, some minor. But in the early 1930's it was becoming obvious that the loops of the big vaudeville circuits were being tightened almost to strangulation, and the "grouch bags" held fewer coins for a rainy day.

Until more and more lavish screen spectacles began to draw in fascinated patrons week after week, stunned theatre managers had not fully realized that the short-reelers they regarded as fillers or chasers, to get rid of crowds which might otherwise have stayed on to see their favorite performers again, foreshadowed the decline of live entertainment. A new medium, radio, offered free performances by vaudeville's top stars to ex-vaudeville patrons stretched out on sofas in the comfort of their living rooms.

Once-bright sketches deteriorated and standards were lowered by the inclusion of untalented performers. Orchestras were transferred from the pit to the stage as featured acts. Other standards were lowered with the advent of a monolithic theatrical combine. It has been claimed that Albee, in endeavoring to monopolize the variety entertainment field, killed it. He lowered the old standards by substituting a five-a-day schedule for the old two-a-day, initiating long runs, and holding over

Two graduates of the "Original Amateur Hour," conducted on radio by Major Bowes and on television by Ted Mack. (Left) Vera Ellen; (right) Regina Resnick, shown with Mr. Mack.

hit headliners—a procedure which gave habitual patrons a surfeit of the same acts. The public expected their comedians served solo, but such performers as Billy Gaxton, Lou Holz, Eddie Cantor, and Georgie Jessel were teamed up as duos and some fans rejected the double portion. Others objected to the new policy of having a master of ceremonies who was free to barge into any spot on the bill, interrupting the routine.

With the opening of vast new theaters like the Roxy and Radio

Red Buttons, a hardy TV perennial, is a graduate of the "Borscht Circuit," an outgrowth of vaudeville.

City Music Hall in New York, vaudeville was all but submerged in elaborate dance numbers, symphony orchestras, and scenic novelties. Nevertheless, the stage presentations usually included an act or two which gave jugglers, mimics, acrobats, and singers a chance to earn a living.

Some vaudeville performers landed roles in Broadway revues, such as the *Ziegfeld Follies, Greenwich Village Follies, The Passing Show,* Earl Carroll's *Vanities,* and Leonard Sillman's *New Faces.*

Radio's popular "Amateur Hour," presided over by Major Bowes, helped keep variety alive during the 1930's by assembling scores of talented performers who had made good on the air into traveling units that appeared in theatres all over the country.

Billy Rose sponsored vaudeville in the star-studded entertainments at his Diamond Horseshoe night club. Luminaries of the past, many of

Danny Kaye set new records when vaudeville was revived at the Palace and his television appearances draw peak ratings.

them down-but-not-out, proved prime magnets for café patrons who had not had a chance to see them in their prime. The Catskill "borscht circuit" of resort hotels also helped keep vaudeville alive and nurtured such versatile performers as Danny Kaye. In this not-so-rustic school for comics, performers had to appear night after night before the same Bronx-Brooklyn vacationers, necessitating a big backlog of snappy new material in order to hold their attention.

Lavish film musical comedies and radio's "canned" music, jokes, wisecracks and extended dramas delivered another broadaxe blow to live specialties. Broadcasting networks offered many entertainers financial lures too alluring to resist, yet somehow the alchemy of showmanship and response often failed when an act which had been a sure-fire success onstage was filtered through cables and monitor screens. The sporadic attempts to rekindle performer-audience rapport via the air waves have at least provided occasional vehicles for the talents of former "greats". Entertainment was to become a catch-all word linked with mammoth benefits, high-priced supper clubs and cabarets or diffused capsules embedded in television spectaculars or Sullivan "shews."

Now and then, of course, a vaudeville performer bobs up in a ball park during intermission—a sad-eyed clown, a buxom comedienne. Industrial and merchandising firms occasionally enliven their conventions and commercial shows for distributors and dealers with vaudeville acts. From time to time local theaters sponsor summer variety shows under the stars and send scores of veteran comics, monologuists, singers and acrobats scurrying to their trunks to dig out old wardrobes and properties.

And, judging by the number of acts which have weathered many seasons of listener- and viewer-ratings, the still-kicking ghost of vaudeville can still hold its own against gyrating torsos, no-nonsense scientific photography which can puncture the mystery and illusions of magicians and the spate of popular songs overflowing every radio and jukebox. Of course a television comedian's livelihood is imperiled by too-frequent performances to the same audience which wear the edge off his humor. How long can any of them continue to supply laughs week after week for a mass audience? In days gone by the public could coddle a joke, but today it hasn't time to savor one between station breaks.

Yet television represents to a degree the timeless triumph of vaudeville. Today any room in which a viewer or a family sit before a set is a theater, and every watcher is his own critic. He has consulted the listing of programs vying for his attention and he has access to previews

Two old vaudevillians, Jack Benny and George Burns, do their stuff for the TV camera along with Bing Crosby.

and reviews in periodicals and to opinions of colleagues, relatives and television repairmen—when he can get hold of one. He knows all, sees all, and, like an insatiable Oliver Twist, asks not only for more but also for better and better fare.

Television has undoubtedly brought about a brave new trend in public rating of entertainment. Although appraisals of the critics still carry weight in the case of new plays and musicals, in the case of television shows the public is first on the scene and usually makes up its own mind as to a plus or minus verdict before reading the critics' evaluations the following day.

Today, television still offers a career for the variety actor, for it gives the neophyte an opportunity to develop through working at all sorts of jobs—announcing, serving as a master of ceremonies, singing or dancing in a chorus or ensemble and, in the process, getting the feel of that vague but important assemblage, the watching audience.

And although television includes many young entertainers who have yet to prove themselves, it has also kept before the public many beloved stars who began their careers as vaudevillians in their youth— Georgie Jessel, Eddie Cantor, Bert Lahr, Jack Benny, Jimmy Durante, Bob Hope, Sophie Tucker, Burns and Allen, Milton Berle and that veteran charmer, Maurice Chevalier. Ed Wynn provides a unique example of the amazing continuity of vaudeville. Still going strong, he appeared on the opening bill of the Palace many years ago, linking the past with the present with or without his outrageous comic garb and guileless "Perfect Fool" smile.

PART TWO
A Gallery of Vaudevillians

Here they are! The performers who made you laugh, hold your breath, weep, sing, whistle and applaud. As you look at your favorites, you will recall their costumes, make-up, gags, fancy stepping and timing.

If only there were space enough to hold all you admired, both great and small! For some, alas, are inevitably missing: child impersonator Ina Claire, imitating Harry Lauder; Herman Timberg; Jack Waldron; Jimmy Hussy; Clarence Nordstrom; the Templeton Brothers; Jerry Bergen; the three Du Four Brothers; and Leo Carillo—to name a few that come to mind.

"Where are the animal acts?" you will complain, "and the cartoonists, Harry Hershfield, 'Mr. New York,' and pseudo-inventor 'Rube' Goldberg? Where are the composers, Leo Edwards and Mabel McKinley, niece of the assassinated president?"

Some are missing who played vaudeville without even your remembering, Marion Davies, who appeared in sketches at the Palace; Jean Dalrymple, who made theatrical history with her revivals of musical and dramas at City Center; and Elsa Maxwell, czarina of the international set, who started her career as a piano accompanist in vaudeville.

What an inexhaustible gallery!

Starting as a dancing act, Fred and Adele Astaire became top stars of Broadway musicals. Subsequently Adele married an English peer and retired from the stage and Fred went on to become the most famous dancer in American show business, with triumphs in movies and television.

The Avon Comedy Four included originally Joe Smith, Charlie Dale, John Coleman and Will Lester. Later replacements were Jack Goodwin and Eddie Miller. The comedy and vocalizing were sure-fire; the performers beloved.

Professor Backwards befuddled delighted audiences with his reverse rules for writing.

Colossal awkwardness and misadventure characterized The Baggage Crashers, extraordinarily funny comedy sketch.

A heart-throb voice and a compelling womanliness made Belle Baker always a favorite of the two-a-day. She was the first woman single to close the show at the Palace.

Phil Baker, the bad boy from the Bronx, was one of the first to employ stooges and to charm the ear with an accordion. He presided over the radio show "Take It or Leave It," the birthplace of the "sixty-four-dollar question."

Mr. and Mrs. Jimmy Barry, excellent exponents of skit with songs and dances.

"He can do anything." This verdict James Barton proved in his youth as a burlesquer, vaudeville and legitimate stage star, who could sing, dance, speak lines and create the funniest drunk that the stage has ever known.

Peg-Leg Bates, whose celerity and skill, in spite of physical handicap, won cheers.

Nora Bayes, billed as "The Greatest Single Woman Singing Comedienne in the World," was as flamboyont off-stage as on. She traveled in a private railway car with a retinue. When she appeared with husband Jack Norworth she insisted on the billing: "NORA BAYES, Assisted and Admired by Jack Norworth."

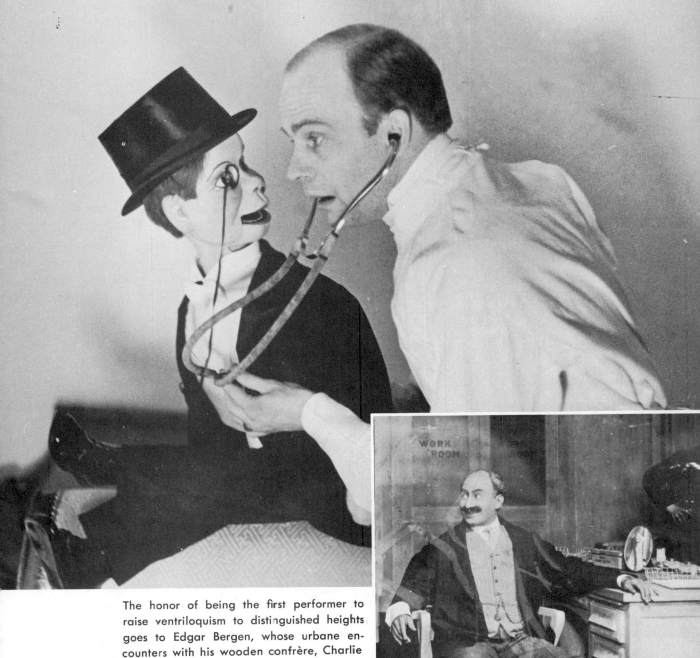

The honor of being the first performer to raise ventriloquism to distinguished heights goes to Edgar Bergen, whose urbane encounters with his wooden confrère, Charlie McCarthy, brought him vaudeville, radio and television fame.

Barney Bernard's dialect comedy led to stardom in the hit play *Potash and Perlmutter*.

His broad comedy and thick German dialect carried
Sam Bernard from a single act to the *Music Box Revue*.

Ben Bernie, who started his career as a boy violinist,
later used the instrument as an idle prop when he
became a famous band leader.

After years of headlining, the beloved comedy team of Block and Sully deserted the footlights for a successful career in the stock market.

The glittering "bird-and-a-bottle" era was headed by "Diamond Jim" Brady, exhibitionist, theatre enthusiast and constant escort of the whilom variety actress, Lillian Russell.

When not appearing with the irrepressible Bert Savoy, Jay Brennan, extraordinary female impersonator, played opposite Stanley Rogers, with whom he is shown in this picture.

The Britons and Rita—a typical acrobatic act.

A burlesque graduate and Follies star, Fanny Brice had variety audiences roaring over her "Dying Swan" dance satire. Later she became nationally famous as the radio brat, Baby Snooks.

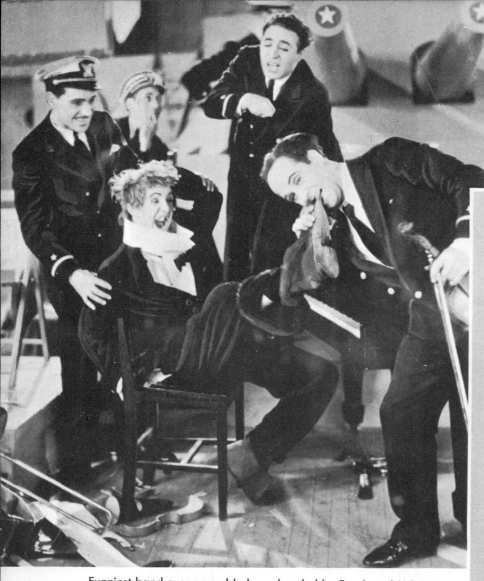

Funniest band ever assembled was headed by Frank and Milt Britton, who ended their act by smashing their instruments and generally turning the stage into a shambles.

Joe Browning, sanctimonious comic, delivering a timely sermon.

As one of the Five Marvelous Ashtons, acrobat Joe E. Brown, famous comic, made his earliest stage bid for attention.

Buck and Bubbles, in "Weather Clear—Track Fast," established a high place for themselves as off-beat comics, smoothie artists whose recurrent engagements always created a storm of fresh applause. As a solo performer, John Bubbles did a noteworthy characterization in *Porgy and Bess.*

In their familiar vaudeville act George Burns first shouldered the comedy and beautiful Gracie Allen served as the somewhat dumb foil. Her tag line was: "Oh, George, I bet you say that to all the girls." Their long association extended into radio and television, with Gracie becoming a modern Mrs. Malaprop.

In his series of revues, called
the "Vanities," Earl Carroll
featured many vaudeville
acts. He was happiest when
serving as a beauty expert,
the role he exploits in this
picture.

As a top woman single act,
Marie Cahill, warbler, had an
enthusiastic following.

Starting as a member of an obscure vaudeville team, Eddie Cantor, "Banjo Eyes," became the hand-clapping, prancing star of the Ziegfeld Follies, *Kid Boots*, radio and television. His autobiographies had a wide sale and his charities were numerous. After Broadway successes, he teamed with George Jessel as a Palace record-breaker.

- HARRY CARROLL -

Expert at "thumping the box" was Harry Carroll who became a successful producer of big musical acts.

Teaming first in burlesque with Paul McCullough, Bobby Clark, one of the great comedians of his era, became a Broadway musical comedy star, climaxing his artistry with the title role in Molière's classic, *Le Bourgeois Gentilhomme*.

Credit for precipitating the national dance craze goes to Irene & Vernon Castle.

That lively night club trio, Clayton (right), Jackson (left), and Durante (center) brought their noisy humor to vaudeville. Then Jimmy Durante broke away from his pals to become a solo radio, cinema, television and revue star.

The Four Cohans on a comedy rampage.

Josephine Cohan left the Four Cohans to do a comedy act with her husband, Fred Niblo.

Droll comedian Willie Collier took time off to do an act with his little boy who became the film star Buster Collier, Jr.

Polished straight man ex-pugilist "Gentleman Jim" Corbett and adroit comic Bobby Barry.

The popular dance team, the Cansinos, Elsa and Eduardo, gained post-theatrical prominence by becoming the parents of Rita Hayworth.